A BEGINNER'S BOOK
OF
VEGETABLE GARDENING

A BEGINNER'S BOOK
OF
VEGETABLE GARDENING

Sigmund A. Lavine

*Illustrated with photographs
and with drawings by Jane O'Regan*

DODD, MEAD & COMPANY · NEW YORK

Illustration Credits

Ames, a McDonough Company, 24, 25, 26, 27 (lower left and right), 28, 119; W. Atlee Burpee Company, 10, 11, 17, 56 (top), 57 (right), 68, 69, 71, 72, 73, 74, 76, 78, 81, 82, 85, 87, 89, 91, 94, 95, 98, 100, 112, 116, 117; Rosemary Casey, 122; Corn Refiners Association, Inc., 12; Dover Stamping Company, 27 (top right); Maine Agriculture Department Photograph, 19; Jane O'Regan, 16 (adapted from Burpee Catalog), 21, 31, 32, 37, 50, 52, 53, 54, 55, 57 (left), 58, 60, 63, 65, 83, 84, 93, 103, 105, 107, 107 (bottom left after Handsaker), 107 (middle and bottom right after White), 108, 108 (bottom left and bottom middle after White), 109, 113, 114, 118; United States Department of Agriculture Photographs, 8 (by Knell), 18, 34, 46, 47, 56 (bottom), 59, 61, 62 (by George C. Pace), 64, 66; United States Department of Agriculture Bulletins, 42–43, 44–45, 49 (#28).

1 2 3 4 5 6 7 8 9 10

Library of Congress Cataloging in Publication Data

Lavine, Sigmund A
A beginner's book of vegetable gardening.

Includes index.
SUMMARY: Discusses all aspects of vegetable gardening from choosing tools and preparing the soil to harvesting the crop.
1. Vegetable gardening—Juvenile literature.
[1. Vegetable gardening. 2. Gardening] I. O'Regan, Jane. II. Title.
SB324.L38   635   76–53439
ISBN 0–396–07410–3

*For—Bob Berry who has planted
the seeds of understanding
among children of all races.*

CONTENTS

Gardening is fun for the entire family.

1

WHY VEGETABLES?

"More grows in the garden than the gardener has sown."

Every year more and more people plant vegetables in their backyards, in window boxes, or in containers on rooftops and terraces. If you ask these individuals why they raise vegetables most of them will give practical reasons. They will probably make two claims. The first is that freshly picked vegetables taste far better than those purchased in stores. Secondly, they will point out that it is cheaper to raise vegetables than to buy them.

There are other practical reasons for having a vegetable garden. Raising vegetables is a worthwhile leisure time outdoor activity in which the whole family can join. Then, too, vegetable gardening teaches the value of patience—Nature will cooperate with a gardener but cannot be rushed by him.

But even if there were no practical reasons for raising vegetables, it would be an enormously rewarding avocation. There is just as great a thrill in growing a well-formed, firm head of lettuce as there is in raising a perfect rose.

Actually, the joy of vegetable gardening is not limited to harvesting delicious vegetables. There's fun in selecting a garden site, choosing tools, examining the packets of seeds displayed in racks in garden shops and, most delightful of all, browsing through seed catalogs. Then, too, there are the quiet pleasures of planning a garden and daydreaming of growing so many vegetables that you have a hard time giving them away.

But in truth, the greatest joy of gardening is sowing seed and caring for

Backyard gardeners not only harvest a crop of delicious vegetables but also reap the pleasure of "making things grow." Green pod snap beans, scallop squash, butternut squash, sweet pepper, corn, tomato, eggplant.

The town-dwelling Indians of North Carolina were America's first back-yard gardeners. This drawing of the town of Secota made in the sixteenth century shows plots of pumpkins, corn, and other crops.

plants from the time they sprout until they are ready to pick. It is not difficult to experience this unique satisfaction. Merely bear in mind that "no mystery is involved in the making of a garden; only the learning of a few of Nature's laws, and the likes and dislikes of plants."

All experienced gardeners frankly admit that even though they faithfully followed the advice given to them by experts, they have, from time to time, raised tough string beans, bitter cucumbers, and stringy beets. Actually, few gardens are complete successes season after season. The most carefully tended garden can be ruined by hot, humid weather or a prolonged rainy spell. But gardeners expect minor misfortunes and consider a crop failure a challenge to have a better garden the following year.

As indicated, vegetable gardening is a most delightful activity. However, reaping a harvest entails work. Unless a plot is properly prepared and planted it will be a waste of time and effort to carry out gardening chores.

2

PLANNING THE GARDEN

"It is a bad plan that cannot be altered."

Most people have little choice in selecting a garden site. Apartment-house dwellers are limited to window ledges, roofs, balconies, and terraces unless they live in communities that provide residents with plots in parks or in vacant lots. All too often these areas are a considerable distance from a would-be gardener's home. But the pleasures of gardening more than compensate for this inconvenience.

Where to Plant

A garden should be as close to one's house as possible. This makes it more convenient to tend to plantings, reduces the chances of destruction by unthinking individuals or stray dogs and cats, and makes it easier for the family cook.

But even homeowners cannot always raise vegetables near their kitchen doors. Ideally, vegetables should receive full sunlight throughout the day. All too frequently the section of a yard that gets the most sun is not suitable for a garden. Then, too, shadows cast by surrounding buildings or trees reduce the amount of sunlight that falls on a garden.

Trees not only block the sun but also compete with crops for the nutrients and water in the soil. Thus a garden should be located as far away from trees as possible. If the only available space is near trees, a garden must be watered frequently and heavily fertilized. Unfortunately, this, in turn, stimulates the roots of the trees—which fan out in all directions—to stretch further into a garden and become even more of a nuisance.

Actually, if you plan to garden beside trees, the best thing to do is to block the invasion by their roots by digging a trench along the sides of the plot, cut off any roots that are exposed, then either fill the trench with concrete or insert a zinc or galvanized barrier in it. This arduous task will greatly increase the productivity of a tree-surrounded garden. Because there is little likelihood that any "main" roots will be severed, the chances of the trees being injured are remote.

If possible, locate your garden on high ground rather than in a low area. This will lessen the danger of losing plants to a late frost—high ground is warmer than low ground. Also try to give your plot a southern exposure. Not only will it be bathed in sunlight much of the day but also it can be planted at least a week earlier than a garden with northern exposure. This is because the soil warms faster.

However, vegetables planted in a garden that gets ample sunlight and has a southern exposure will not thrive without topsoil—the dark surface layer that contains organic matter. Nor will vegetables prosper where the soil consists of clay or hardpan. Clay becomes sticky in rainy weather and "bakes" during hot spells. Hardpan (a cementlike soil) is so compacted that it does not permit drainage nor can vegetable roots penetrate it.

But don't abandon the idea of having a garden even if the only available area has a scant layer of topsoil over clay or hardpan. Sand and cinders will open the texture of compacted subsoil, while topsoil can be enriched and increased by the addition of compost, humus, and manure. Directions for improving poor soil and making good soil even better are given on page 31.

You will be extremely lucky if your backyard is an ideal garden site. So use whatever space is available and adapt your planting to its flaws and faults. For example, if your plot slopes so steeply that heavy rains are apt to wash out plants, run the rows sideways across the pitch.

How Large a Garden?

Obviously, available space determines a garden's size. But bear in mind that the larger the garden, the more work it entails. Unless they have

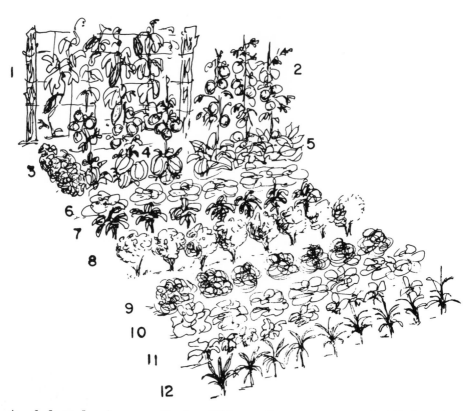

A salad garden in a small plot. This garden measures only 10 feet by 15 feet, yet it offers a surprising variety of tasty salad vegetables: 1. Cucumber, 2. cherry tomato, 3. dwarf parsley, 4. green pepper, 5. zucchini, 6. cabbage, 7. beet, 8. carrot, 9. curled endive, 10. lettuce, 11. radish, 12. sweet Spanish onion.

decided to have a small garden, novices should curb their enthusiasm and plant an area only half as big as the one they would like to cultivate. A bountiful harvest of carrots, cucumbers, beets, swiss chard, lettuce, tomatoes, and beans can be reaped from a plot measuring only six feet by eight feet. The secret is to train the beans, cucumbers, and tomatoes to grow vertically.

Of course, if you plan to spend all your leisure time working in a garden you can have a much larger one than an individual who considers gardening a part-time summer activity. Nor will a large garden prove a burden if an entire family shares the task of caring for it. But if a garden is to be the

Training vine crops and pole beans to climb a wire trellis will save space in a small garden.

sole responsibility of one person who has other interests, it should be a small one. Then, if experience proves that a bigger garden will not demand more time and energy than they are willing to devote to it, they can enlarge their plot the following season.

Perhaps the best way to avoid planting more crops than one can properly care for is to remember that it is impossible to grow everything from asparagus to zucchini in the average backyard. However, this is usually most difficult to remember when examining seed catalogs with their attractive colored illustrations. Therefore, besides considering how much attention you are willing to give a garden, don't fail to take into account that vegetables differ in their requirements. Also be mindful that the yield from some vegetables is greatly disproportionate to the amount of room they

TABLE 1

Kind of Vegetable	Seed or Plants required for 25 foot row		Number of Inches Between		Approximate Days to	
	Seed	Plants	Rows	Plants	Germinate	Maturity
Beans						
Bush	1/4 lb.		24–30	2–4	4–8	40–65
*Pole	1/8 lb.		30–36	6–8	4–8	60–75
Lima (bush)	1/4 lb.		24–30	4–6	4–8	60–75
*Lima (pole)	1/8 lb.		30–36	6–8	4–8	75–100
Beet	1/2 oz.		12–15	3–4	6–10	50–60
Broccoli		20	24–30	15	4–8	60–100
Cabbage		20	24–30	15	4–8	65–120
Carrot	1/8 oz.		12–15	3–4	10–15	65–80
Cauliflower		20	24–30	15	4–8	80–110
*Corn	1/16 lb.		30–36	6–8	6–8	65–100
*Cucumber	1/8 oz.		60–72	12–15	6–10	70–80
Eggplant		12	30–36	24	10–15	100–120
Lettuce						
Head	1/16 oz.		12–15	8–12	4–8	50–75
Leaf	1/16 oz.		12–15	2–4	4–8	30–35
*Melon	1/8 oz.		60–72	6–8	8–10	75–100
Onion Seed	1/4 oz.		12–15	3–5	6–12	120–155
Sets	1/2 lb.		12–15	3–5		60–80
Parsley	1/16 oz.		12–15	4–6	15–25	80–90
Parsnip	1/8 oz.		12–18	3–4	12–20	120–150
Peas	1/4 lb.		24–30	1–2	8–12	60–90
Peppers		20	18–30	15	6–10	100–120
*Potato	21 lbs.		30–36	15–18	8–12	90–115
*Pumpkin	1/4 oz.		72–84	15–16	4–8	75–110
Radish	1/4 oz.		6–12	1–2	4–8	25–35
Spinach	1/4 oz.		10–15	2–3	6–10	50–70
Squash						
Bush	1/8 oz.		36–42	24–36	4–8	50–60
*Vine	1/8 oz.		84–96	18–21	4–8	90–110
Swiss Chard	1/4 oz.		12–15	4–5	6–10	30–40
Tomato						
Staked		20	30–36	12–18	18	78–110
Unstaked		12	30–36	20–26	48–60	78–110
Turnip	1/16 oz.		12–15	3–4	4–8	40–80

*Planted in hills

Because of their high yield, potatoes justify the space they require. The colorful blossoms also add beauty to a vegetable garden.

demand. For example, the weight of sweet corn harvested from a one-hundred-foot row is about fifteen pounds. A row of equal length will furnish approximately one hundred pounds of tomatoes. Both seed catalogs and seed packets mention the space required for specific vegetables.

Make a Plan

A garden plan will not guarantee a bountiful harvest, but it will insure that space will not be wasted and that every plant will have room to develop. The careful planning of a garden will also make it continuously productive all through the growing season. Moreover, a plan enables one to take full advantage of the favorable features of a garden site. Thus if there is an unshaded wall or fence near your plot, include it in your plan. Vine crops—particularly cucumbers—are easily trained to climb. This not only saves space but also increases the production of clean, well-formed fruit because the cucumbers do not come in contact with the ground. Pole beans and peas can also be supported by a fence or wall.

Before making a plan on graph paper—let each square represent one square foot—verify the space requirements of the crops you wish to grow. Also take into consideration the amount of time needed for them to mature. Then, indicate the placement of the various plantings on the plan.

Personal preferences and the size and shape of a garden make every garden plan different, but there are a few fundamental rules. One section of the plot should be devoted to beets, carrots, and other root crops that

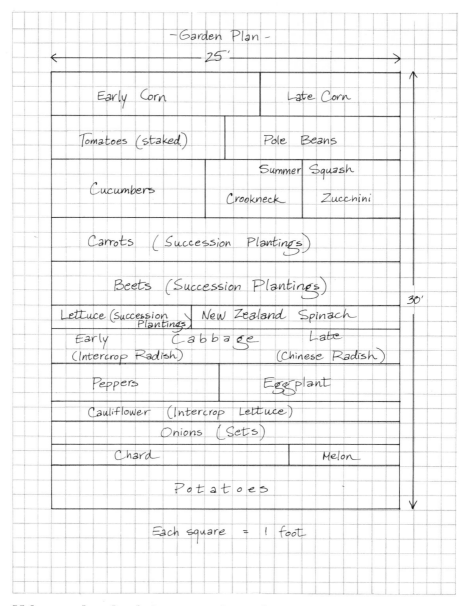

-Garden Plan -

←————————————— 25' —————————————→

| Early Corn | Late Corn |

Tomatoes (staked) | Pole Beans

Cucumbers | Summer Squash
| Crookneck | Zucchini

Carrots (Succession Plantings)

Beets (Succession Plantings)

Lettuce (Succession Plantings) | New Zealand Spinach

Early Cabbage Late
(Intercrop Radish) (Chinese Radish)

Peppers | Eggplant

Cauliflower (Intercrop Lettuce)

Onions (Sets)

Chard | Melon

P o t a t o e s

30'

Each square = 1 foot

Make a garden plan *before* you order seeds.

can be sown as soon as the ground can be worked. Grouping root crops enables a gardener to completely plant part of his plot at a very early date.

Another rule decrees that a plan should show plantings placed according to the respective heights of vegetables. Thus corn and pole beans should be grown on one side of a garden. If planted in the middle of a plot they will cast shadows on low-growing vegetables. Incidentally, if possible, plan to run all rows north and south so that every plant will get the same amount of sunlight. No matter how the rows run, they should be straight. Vegetables do not grow better in straight rows than in crooked ones but straight rows are far easier to cultivate.

A plan should show the use of lettuce as a companion crop. Because lettuce matures quickly it can be planted between broccoli, cabbage, and tomatoes, or sown between the rows of other slow-growing vegetables. This space-saving technique is called intercropping.

Experienced plan-makers always provide for succession planting. This is done in two ways. The first is to sow a rapidly maturing vegetable in the

MAY 30

PLANTED 6 BONNIE BEST TOMATO SEEDLINGS

JUNE 6
CUTWORMS GOT TWO ☹ (USE COLLARS NEXT YEAR!)

AUGUST 9
FIRST FRUIT PICKED PLANT ON OTHER SIDE OF GARDEN NEXT YEAR (MORE SUN!)

If you keep a log of your gardening activities and record your successes and failures, it will help you plan future gardens.

same row from which a slow-growing crop is to be harvested. This trick makes the maximum use of garden space.

The second method insures a summer-long supply of those vegetables that have a short growing season. It consists of frequent plantings of short rows. If seed is sown at seven- to ten-day intervals—the planting dates are shown on the plan—the second sowing will be ready to pick just as the last of the original crop is harvested. Meanwhile, a third planting will be developing while the first row can be replanted.

Never discard a garden plan after it has been used. It will prove invaluable for reference, particularly if you raise members of the cabbage family. These vegetables are subject to soil-borne diseases unless rotated—planted in a different part of a garden—every year. Actually, because of the varying demands vegetables make on soil, it is a good practice—although unnecessary, if a garden is well fertilized—to rotate all crops.

Recording varieties planted, the amount of seed sown, planting and harvesting dates, and brief comments on successes and failures in a notebook will make planning future gardens easier. Moreover, your notes will prevent you from making the same mistakes.

3

TOOLS

"A tool is but the extension of a man's hand."

Very few tools are needed for successful gardening, but those you have should be of the highest quality. Although tools with hardwood handles and fashioned from heavy-gauge steel are more expensive than the lighter, cheaply made ones, they are a much better investment. Top-grade gardening accessories last for years, holding their cutting edges, and do not bend, break, or splinter easily.

Novice gardeners are always tempted to purchase fancy gadgets displayed in garden supply shops that supposedly make gardening a simple task. However, none of these devices—many of which have little value—should be bought until one has acquired the following:

Hoe. This flat-bladed, long-handled tool is invaluable to the gardener. It is used to break up clods, level soil, make furrows, cultivate (loosen the ground around plants), and to "chop" weeds.

Hose. Although vegetables can be watered with an ordinary hose or sprinkler, neither is as efficient as a "soil soaker"—a porous canvas hose which is laid between the rows to saturate the surrounding area slowly.

Rake. The best type of rake is the steel bow variety which resembles "an oversized comb on a long handle." Rakes that have brackets running from the bar above the teeth to either side of the handle are best. The brackets give added strength to a tool that is sure to be wracked by roots, rocks, and debris while soil is being loosened and smoothed for planting.

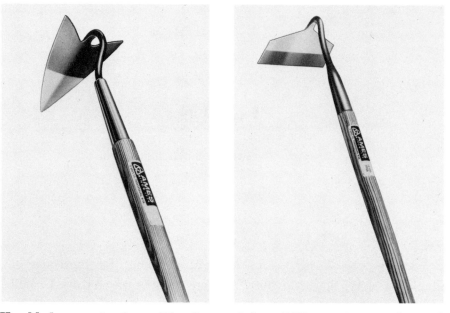

Hoe blades vary in shape. The diamond-shaped Warren hoe can be used to make furrows as well as to "chop" weeds, while both the squared-top onion hoe and the socket-pattern beet hoe make cultivation of crops a simple task. If you are going to purchase only one hoe, choose one with a wide carbon steel blade and a hardwood handle (bottom right).

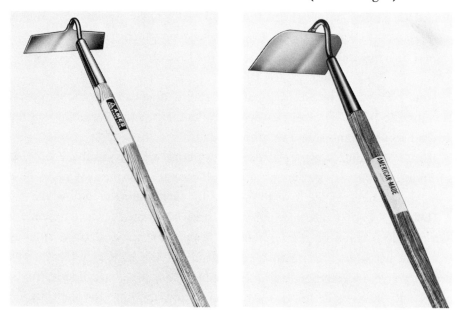

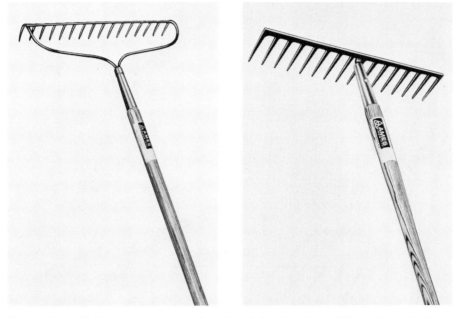

Bow rakes (left) are stronger than level head rakes. Those forged from one piece of steel will prove more satisfactory than welded ones. Some gardeners prefer straight teeth on a level head rake (right) like the one pictured here. Others consider curved teeth more efficient.

Spading Fork.   Unless a garden is large enough to justify plowing it with machinery, a spading fork is needed to turn over soil and to break up clods before the ground is raked.

Sprayer.   No matter how much pleasure one derives from a garden, destructive insects may enjoy it even more. While birds and beneficial insects help control pests, most gardeners resort to chemicals to destroy "bugs." These preparations are applied to vegetable plants with either a hand sprayer or a duster. The former is used for liquid insecticides, the latter for dry poisons. Detailed instructions for combating insects are given in Chapter 7.

Trowel.   Although designed for moving small plants, this scoop-shaped tool can be used to cultivate, spread fertilizer and lime, dig weeds, and pry up small roots. All-metal trowels will take more punishment than those with wooden handles, but some people find them uncomfortable. Better test the "feel" of both types before making a purchase.

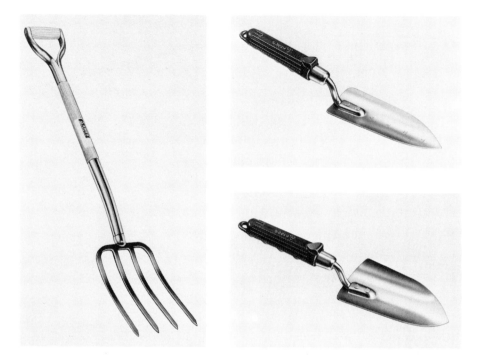

A four-tined fork (left) is an indispensable tool for the gardener. It is used to turn over soil, break up clods, and pry up stones. (Right) Two types of trowels. The one on the top was designed for transplanting. Note the figures on the blade, which indicate inches.

Twine. A length of heavy twine tightly tied to two sturdy stakes insures straight rows if stretched taut and used as a guide when making furrows. The stakes also can be employed to measure the distance between rows if you daub a paint mark along each foot of their length.

Watering Can. A watering can (a necessity for container gardeners) simplifies the application of liquid fertilizers. It can also be used to give individual plants a "drink" and to dampen the soil around transplants.

Well-maintained tools not only last longer but they are also more efficient. It is far easier and faster to cultivate with a sharp hoe than with a dull one. But the start of the gardening season is not the time to put tools in shape. This chore should be done in the autumn. Before putting tools away for the winter, all soil sticking to them should be removed by scrubbing

A sprinkling can makes the application of water soluble fertilizers an easy task. It also can be used to water transplants and mist sowings of seeds.

A round-pointed shovel (left) is a most useful garden tool. Manufacturers offer two types: one has a short handle, the other has a handle approximately four feet long. It is easy to dig with a hollow-backed shovel (right) made with foot saving forward turned steps and a serrated blade.

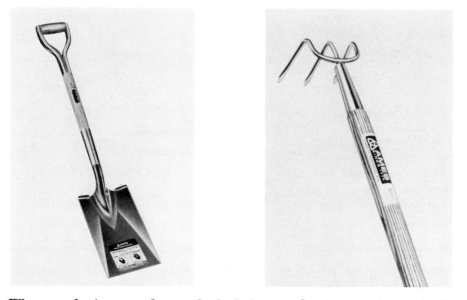

When purchasing a garden spade, look for one that has metal completely covering the fork (above left). This will protect the wood from moisture and eliminates weathering. A three-tined "floral" cultivator (right) will break up compacted soil and unroot weeds. A gardener's delight—a cultivator-weeder hoe (below left). It does two jobs at once. Here's a most practical gadget, a two-pronged weeding hoe (right) that can be used either to scuff weeds or dig them out of the ground.

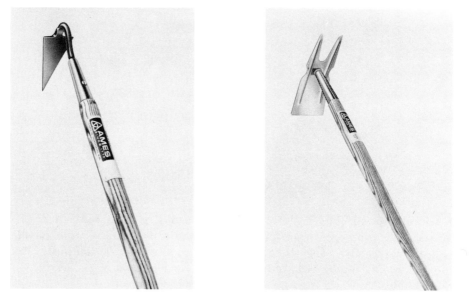

with water and a stiff wire brush. When the tools are clean, wipe them dry. If handles are no longer smooth, painful splinters can be avoided by sand-papering the wood. Minor cracks in handles can be repaired either by wrapping them tightly with wire or with electrician's tape.

After tools have been cleaned, mended, and their cutting edges sharp-ened, cover both their metal and wooden parts with a thin coat of oil applied with a soft cloth. Oil removed from lawn mowers is excellent for this purpose. So is the oil drained from automobiles. The latter can be secured at any service station. Note: Unless you own a grinding wheel and a collec-tion of files and have mastered the use of these tools, send your gardening implements with cutting edges to a professional for sharpening.

4

SOIL AND PREPARATION

"Earth, the giver of grain"

All soil is made up of varying proportions of clay, gravel, sand, minute particles of rock (silt), and organic matter called humus. Vegetables do best in loam—a rock-free soil composed of about 10 percent silt and approximately equal parts of sand, clay, and humus. Generally speaking, vegetables prefer loam that is slightly acid.

Each of loam's components has properties vital to plant growth. Clay is rich in nutrients, sand provides drainage and aeration, silt prevents the leeching (draining) out of moisture and plant foods. Humus is the most important ingredient. It lightens soil, holds moisture, and furnishes food to the bacteria that turn organic materials into the nitrates needed by plants.

Anyone who knows how to make a snowball can find out whether or not the "dirt" in his garden is loam. If a moist handful of soil packs readily and forms a hard ball, it contains a high percentage of clay. Soil that cannot be molded into a ball is mostly sand. But soil that balls easily, yet breaks apart when slight pressure is applied, is loam.

The chances are your soil contains too much sand or clay to be classified as loam. However, sandy loam is an excellent medium for raising vegetables. It drains quickly, dries rapidly after a rain, is a good transplanting vehicle, and is easy to cultivate or weed. But soil with a very high sand content is not fertile and, the coarser the sand, the faster it drains—a serious problem in dry spells. Clay soils have no favorable features. They are best described as being the opposite of sandy loam.

30

Example of stratification of the soil: 1. loamy soil, few pebbles; 2. coarser soil, pebbles, stones, clay, and dirt; 3. clay.

Fortunately, all soil can be turned into good garden loam. Adding various types of humus—peat moss, well-rotted manure, decomposed seaweed, or other organic material—will improve soil containing too much sand. Humus and sharp sand (available from suppliers of building materials) turn compacted soils into loam. But don't attempt to guess how much sand or humus should be used to change soil structure. Instead, send a sample of your soil to the nearest office of the Agricultural Extension Service. The Service, a unit of the United States Department of Agriculture, will test the soil sample scientifically and give specific instructions for improving your soil.

If the Service finds your soil too acid, it will recommend the use of lime. Therefore, along with the sample, give the Service the measurements of your garden and a list of the crops you intend to grow. This information will enable the experts to advise how much dolomitic limestone or agricultural lime your garden requires.

Because lime takes a considerable time to "break down," it is best worked into the soil in the fall. Never apply more lime than is needed. Too much lime may prevent plants from benefitting from nutrients in the soil.

In addition to following the suggestions of the Agricultural Service, you can enrich soil in other ways. One method is to plant winter rye as a "cover crop." Winter rye will prevent topsoil from being blown away and also will enrich the soil if it is turned under the following spring. Sow winter rye in early autumn. The seed—a half-pound for each hundred square feet—should be broadcast (scattered in all directions) over the garden and then scratched into the ground with a rake.

Mulches—layers of organic materials such as lawn clippings, leaves,

Broadcasting a cover crop in the fall and turning it under the following spring adds humus to the soil. In addition, the plants' roots will prevent erosion when the snow melts.

hay, and sawdust—used to keep down weeds and to retain moisture, should not be discarded at the end of the growing season. If worked into the soil, bacteria will transform them into humus.

Old rotted manure will also improve soil structure. Fresh manure—which contains more plant food than rotted manure—also makes soil richer and more friable (easily pulverized). However, fresh manure burns plant roots. Therefore it should be applied several weeks before planting time. This will give the manure time to "cool." Meanwhile, the soil will be storing up certain of the foods needed by vegetables as it absorbs the leeched nutrients.

Compost

Not only is the percentage of humus in the average garden soil quite low but also the amount available to plants becomes progressively less each time a plot is planted. As a result, if you plan to cultivate the same area year after year, it is absolutely necessary that you increase your soil's humus content.

This task is not as simple as it once was. When barnyard manures were readily secured, neither professional nor amateur gardeners had to worry about soil structure. Barnyard manures are first-rate sources of humus as well as being excellent fertilizers. Today, the automobile has taken the place of the horse and housing developments have replaced suburban dairy and chicken farms, making barnyard manures increasingly difficult to obtain.

To take their place, backyard gardeners have borrowed the Old World technique of making humus rich in plant foods by decomposing organic material under controlled conditions. This process is known as composting. The humus derived thus is called compost.

Have you ever dug for earthworms in the woods? If so, you probably noticed that underneath the mat of partially decayed organic materials the soil was fine and dark. This is because all dead vegetation and the leaves, twigs, branches, and trees that fall to the ground eventually rot and are turned into humus by bacteria. Composting is an imitation of nature's method of manufacturing humus rich in plant foods.

The simplest way of composting consists of making a mound of alternate layers of soil and organic materials and leaving the pile to decompose without any attention until it has been transformed into humus. This may take as long as three years. However, if fertilizers and lime are added to the layers and the pile is kept uniformly moist, humus can be produced in far less time.

But don't expect a compost pile to magically change garbage, garden refuse, lawn clippings, sawdust, and leaves into humus overnight. Very little decomposition will take place when the temperature drops below 45°F. It takes between six and eight months of warm weather to break down fine organic matter such as lawn clippings. Coarse materials take twice as long.

A compost pile should be located in the shade where it can be easily watered. The first step is to dig a shallow pit about eight inches deep. To keep the pile compact, surround the excavation with an enclosure made of cement blocks, chicken wire, or wood. If cement blocks or wood are used, leave spaces so air will reach the pile. Soil bacteria cannot incorporate organic material into humus without air. While a chicken wire fence provides ample ventilation, all compost piles should be turned over occasionally. This not only aerates them but also gives the compost an even texture.

Build up the pile by arranging organic waste in layers (avoid fat, bones, and coffee grounds as they take a very long time to decompose). Layers of coarse material should be about ten inches high, those made up of fine matter half as deep. Cover each layer with five pounds of an all-purpose commercial fertilizer, a handful of lime, and two inches of soil. The fertilizer provides food for bacteria, the lime counteracts the acidity of garbage, and the soil keeps the organic material from blowing away.

Because bacterial action will not take place without moisture, sprinkle each layer as it is added to the pile. Depress the top of the pile to catch rain. During dry spells a pile must be watered. But take pains not to soak it. Overwatering may create an unpleasant stench. There is no offensive odor to a properly prepared and cared for compost pile.

Placing a waterproof covering over a compost pile will prevent nutrients from leeching into the ground during prolonged rainy spells.

Besides making composting materials odorous, overwatering will leech valuable plant foods out of a pile's base. This also happens during protracted rains. To prevent the loss of nutrients in foul weather, throw plastic sheeting, canvas, or some other covering over the compost.

When a pile is about four feet high start another. It is also best to begin a new pile every year. Otherwise, humus ready for use cannot be separated from undecomposed materials.

Fertilizer

Vegetable plants have huge appetites. They require sixteen different foods to develop properly. Vegetables, like other vegetation, absorb three foods—carbon, hydrogen, and oxygen—from the air. All the others are found in soil. They are assimilated in solution by the roots.

As indicated, all soils vary in the amount of plant foods they contain. Nevertheless, most garden soils include an ample supply of the majority of the nutrients needed by vegetables. But soil is usually deficient in the three most important plant foods: nitrogen, phosphorus, and potassium. When testing reveals that there is not enough of these three elements in soil to meet plants' demands, they must be furnished by fertilizing.

Although nitrogen, phosphorus, and potassium do not improve soil structure, they make plants more productive. This is because each of the three performs a function vital to the growth and development of all vegetation.

Nitrogen stimulates plant growth. If nitrogen is lacking, plants are scrawny and bear pale-green leaves that turn yellow, then drop. Because four-fifths of the earth's atmosphere is nitrogen, all leaves would be a lush green if plants could draw directly on the nitrogen carried into the soil by rain and snow. But atmospheric nitrogen has to be converted into forms suitable for plant growth before vegetation can ingest it. This fixation is carried out by the same type of bacteria that transforms organic wastes into humus.

Gardeners have nicknamed phosphorus "the root-maker." There is good reason. Plants hungry for phosphorus have poorly developed root systems. They also are stunted and their leaves, like those of vegetation suffering from a lack of nitrogen, turn yellow. However, when the yellowing is due to insufficient phosphorus, the leaves have red or purple blotches on their tips and, in time, the outer edges of the foliage are similarly hued.

Potassium is "the flower-maker." It also regulates the size and coloration of root and vine crops, helps plants resist disease, and aids them in withstanding drought and sudden drops in temperature. When vegetables suffer from a lack of potassium they fail to make normal growth, have weak stems, and, if they bear flowers, the blossoms are small and pale.

Professional growers of asparagus, cabbage, lettuce, and other vegetables that make a heavy top growth fertilize their fields with large amounts of nitrogen. Similarly, individuals who raise carrots, potatoes, and other root crops for market add potassium to their soil. But using several different fertilizers is not practical for the amateur. Few backyard gardeners devote the major part of their plots to one type of crop. Because both root and leafy vegetables are raised in the average garden, a complete fertilizer is best.

Complete fertilizers derive their name from their composition. If you examine a bag of complete fertilizer you'll find that it is stamped with three numbers. This indicates an analysis of the bag's contents. A hundred-pound bag of complete fertilizer bearing the figures 5-10-10 contains five pounds of nitrogen, ten pounds of phosphorus, and ten pounds of potassium. Inert substances and minor nutrients make up the rest of the bag's weight.

Fertilizer manufacturers compound a number of formulas consisting of varying percentages of the three basic plant foods. But irrespective of their composition, complete fertilizers are designed to provide plants grown in unbalanced soil with all the nourishment they require. However, the correct formula must be used. It is a waste of time and money to fertilize with a high potassium mixture if additional nitrogen is needed. While examining leaves and roots will enable you to tell if your plants are receiving a proper diet, it is far wiser to make sure they will before sowing seed.

Unless a soil test reveals that your garden poses special problems, fertilize with 5-10-10. Working four pounds of this mixture into every hundred square feet of garden area will furnish all the nitrogen, phosphorus, and potassium required by most vegetables.

Side-dressing

To give lettuce and other leafy crops a boost, you can safely spread additional fertilizer where you plan to plant them. This will give seedlings plenty of nitrogen, which is most important during early growth. The extra phosphorus and potassium will do no harm. However, don't use a complete fertilizer with a high nitrogen content (10-6-4) unless it is needed. Too much nitrogen will cause vine crops to develop large, lush leaves but the plants will "set" (form) little fruit.

Established vegetable plants should be side-dressed. This consists of scattering a complete fertilizer along both sides of the rows—about a pound for each hundred feet. Don't try to get the fertilizer close to the plants. Not only is there a danger that the fertilizer will burn them but also it is unnecessary. Vegetables have extensive root systems—those of tomatoes may extend as much as five feet in all directions—so that root hairs can find and absorb moisture and nutrients.

It is a good practice to side-dress crops growing in sandy loam with frequent light applications of fertilizer. Because of its structure, sandy loam retains neither moisture nor nutrients. As a result, fertilizer quickly leeches through it.

Instead of side-dressing, some gardeners water the soil around vegetables with a weak solution of a complete fertilizer. However, it is difficult to determine if the solution is too weak to be of value or so strong that it will

Top-dressing

burn the roots. To be safe, this type of fertilizing should be done with one of the soluble plant foods sold in liquid or crystal form. The directions for its use should be carefully followed. Incidentally, soluble plant foods are excellent "starter solutions" when transferring tomatoes, peppers, and other greenhouse-grown plants from flats to the garden.

An ever-growing number of gardeners are convinced that bone meal, cottonseed meal, fish scraps, seaweed, and other natural materials are far better fertilizers than those manufactured by man. Such individuals maintain that "organic gardening" produces healthier plants and more nutritious vegetables.

The debate between the champions of chemical fertilizers and the advocates of organic gardening has become more heated in recent years. However, both groups agree that organic fertilizers not only improve soil structure but also supply plants with nutrients over a much longer period than do chemicals.

5

PLANTING THE GARDEN

"This rule in gardening ne'er forget
To sow dry and set wet."

Selecting Seeds

Vegetable seeds can be purchased in hardware stores, supermarkets, garden supply centers, and other retail outlets. While this is convenient, there are several advantages to buying seeds by mail. The majority of mail-order seed houses raise their own seeds. Proud of their products, they unconditionally guarantee they will prove satisfactory. While certain "rack" suppliers will also refund the purchase price of seeds that disappoint buyers, in general it is far easier to receive an adjustment from a mail-order seed firm.

Buying seeds by mail also gives one a wider choice. Firms that sell seeds by mail usually have plant experts on their staffs who engage in research designed to develop new strains of vegetables whose yield and quality surpass that of standard varieties. These so-called "introductions" are not offered to the public immediately. They are first grown on experimental farms in various regions to determine how they produce under different climatic conditions. No new variety is sold until it has proven itself. Thus, when dealing with a mail-order seed firm, you can either buy "old-fashioned" strains or new ones that are highly recommended.

Finally, mail-order seed firms furnish their customers with copiously illustrated catalogs. In most cases, these publications are not merely lists of seeds but are crammed with valuable suggestions for the planting, cultivation, and care of crops of all kinds.

Most seed catalogs are free. They can be obtained by writing to firms that advertise in garden magazines or in the garden section of newspapers. Incidentally, once you place an order for seeds, you will be sent a catalog every year.

Before catalogs arrive in midwinter you should have your garden plan completed and know how much seed you need. But gardening is not an exact science—if the weather turns wet and cold, seeds rot, while late frosts nip seedlings. Therefore, when compiling your order, make allowance for replanting. If needed, the extra seed will permit resowing with the least possible loss of time. Seed not used can usually be planted another year.

However, it does not pay to save onion, parsley, or parsnip seeds. They are short-lived. On the other hand, bean, brussels sprout, cabbage, carrot, cauliflower, lettuce, pepper, radish, spinach, and turnip seeds have a life of three years. Beet, cucumber, eggplant, muskmelon, and tomato seeds are even longer lived, retaining their vitality for five years.

Don't let your enthusiasm for gardening influence your seed order. The growing season in New England is far too short to permit a thirty-five-pound watermelon to mature. But New Englanders can grow a small, extra early, very productive watermelon bred for northern gardens. In short, only buy seeds of crops that will thrive in your area. Also note whether a variety is "early," "midseason," or "late." All three types have valuable characteristics but early varieties have the advantage of maturing quickly. As a result, a second crop can be sown except in extreme northern regions.

If, after reading seed catalogs, you still are not sure which seeds to buy, ask an experienced gardener in your neighborhood for help. Gardeners delight in sharing their knowledge and experience. Other sources of information are your state's Agricultural Experimental Station (see page 123) or county agricultural agent.

Given a choice, always buy disease-resistant strains. They are identified both in catalog descriptions and by marked packages. There is no greater disappointment for a gardener than to lose a seemingly healthy stand of cucumbers to mosaic (virus disease) or mildew or to see a row of cabbage turn yellow and wilt. Therefore try to select seeds that have been developed to withstand plant diseases or have been treated with chemicals as a protection against infection.

When to Plant

Because vegetable plants vary in their sensitivity to heat and cold, weather determines when seeds should be sown. For example, cold-resistant vegetables that prefer cool weather will not do well if planted during late spring in the southern two-thirds of the United States. But they thrive if sown in early autumn when the weather in that area becomes cooler.

In order to try to extend the growing season in cool regions, gardeners sometimes sow seeds of vegetables susceptible to cold too early. If they are lucky, by the time the seedlings emerge, temperatures are higher. But all too often the seeds rot, making it necessary to replant.

No chances can be taken with warm weather crops. This is particularly true of crops raised in greenhouses or in hotbeds. The slightest chill will kill or stunt them. Thus warm weather crops should not be transplanted into the open until there is no danger of frost.

By referring to Tables 2A and 2B and the maps on pages 42–47, gardeners throughout the United States can determine safe planting times. The maps indicate the average date of the last killing frost in spring and the first killing frost in the fall. But there are limits to the map's accuracy. Weather, despite the use of scientific apparatus, is apt to be unpredictable. Spring may be "late" or "early" in any given year. Then, too, because of geographical features such as lakes, valleys, or mountains, the temperatures of nearby areas often vary greatly. For example, large bodies of water absorb and lose heat very slowly. Therefore a gardener living near a lake may be able to plant his garden as much as two weeks earlier than a gardener residing in a valley.

Another factor that frost maps do not take into consideration is the location of a garden. Late spring or early autumn frosts rarely harm crops planted on slopes. On the other hand, unprotected gardens in the open or in depressions are likely to suffer damage on those nights when forecasters predict "scattered frost in exposed areas."

Nevertheless, irrespective of the location of their gardens and their

TABLE 2A.—Earliest dates, and range of dates, for safe spring planting of vegetables in the open

Crop	Planting dates for localities in which average date of last freeze is—						
	Jan. 30	Feb. 8	Feb. 18	Feb. 28	Mar. 10	Mar. 20	Mar. 30
Asparagus[1]	Feb. 1–Apr. 15	Feb. 10–May 1	Mar. 1–May 1	Mar. 15–June 1	Jan. 1–Mar. 1	Feb. 1–Mar. 10	Feb. 15–Mar. 20.
Beans, lima	Feb. 1–Apr. 15	Feb. 1–May 1	Mar. 1–May 1	Mar. 15–June 1	Mar. 20–June 1	Apr. 1–June 15	Apr. 15–June 20.
Beans, snap	Jan. –Mar. 15	Feb. 1–May 1	Jan. 20–Apr. 1	Feb. 1–Apr. 15	Mar. 15–June 1	Mar. 15–May 25	Apr. 1–June 1.
Beet	Jan. 1–30	Jan. 1–30	Jan. 15–Feb. 15	Feb. 1–Mar. 15	Feb. 15–Mar. 15	Feb. 15–Mar. 15	Mar. 1–20.
Broccoli, sprouting[1]	Jan. 1–30	Jan. 1–30	Jan. 15–Feb. 15	Feb. 1–Mar. 1	Feb. 15–Mar. 15	Feb. 15–Mar. 15	Mar. 1–20.
Brussels sprouts[1]	Jan. 1–15	Jan. 1–Feb. 10	Jan. 1–Feb. 25	Jan. 15–Feb. 25	Jan. 25–Mar. 1	Feb. 1–Mar. 1	Feb. 15–Mar. 10.
Cabbage[1]	(²)	(²)	(²)	(²)	(²)	(²)	(²)
Cabbage, Chinese	Jan. 1–Mar. 1	Jan. 1–Mar. 1	Jan. 15–Mar. 15	Feb. 1–Mar. 15	Feb. 10–Mar. 15	Feb. 15–Mar. 15	Mar. 1–Apr. 10.
Carrot	Jan. 1–Feb. 1	Jan. 1–Mar. 1	Jan. 15–Mar. 1	Feb. 1–Mar. 1	Feb. 10–Mar. 1	Feb. 15–Mar. 15	Mar. 1–Apr. 10.
Cauliflower[1]	Jan. 1–Feb. 1	Jan. 1–Feb. 1	Jan. 1–Feb. 10	Jan. 20–Feb. 20	Feb. 1–Mar. 1	Feb. 10–Mar. 10	Mar. 25–Apr. 15.
Celery and celeriac	Jan. 1–Feb. 1	Jan. 10–Feb. 10	Feb. 1–20	Feb. 1–Mar. 1	Feb. 20–Mar. 20	Mar. 1–Apr. 1	Mar. 15–Apr. 15.
Chard	Jan. 1–Apr. 1	Jan. 1–Apr. 1	Jan. 20–Apr. 15	Feb. 1–May 1	Feb. 20–May 15	Mar. 20–May 1	Mar. 1–May 25.
Chervil and chives	Jan. 1–Feb. 1	Jan. 1–Feb. 1	Jan. 1–Feb. 1	Jan. 15–Feb. 15	Feb. 1–Mar. 1	Feb. 15–Mar. 15	Feb. 15–Mar. 15.
Chicory, witloof					June 1–July 1	June 1–July 1	June 1–July 1.
Collards[1]	Jan. 1–Feb. 15	Jan. 1–Feb. 15	Jan. 1–Mar. 15	Jan. 15–Mar. 15	Feb. 1–Apr. 1	Feb. 15–May 1	Mar. 1–June 1.
Cornsalad	Jan. 1–Feb. 15	Jan. 1–Mar. 15	Jan. 1–Mar. 15	Jan. 15–Mar. 15	Jan. 1–Mar. 15	Jan. 15–Mar. 15	Mar. 25–Mar. 15.
Corn, sweet	Jan. 1–Feb. 1	Jan. 1–Feb. 1	Feb. 1–Mar. 15	Feb. 15–Apr. 15	Mar. 10–Apr. 15	Mar. 15–May 1	Mar. 1–Apr. 1.
Cress, upland	Jan. 1–Feb. 1	Jan. 1–Feb. 1	Jan. 15–Feb. 15	Feb. 1–Mar. 1	Feb. 15–Apr. 15	Feb. 20–Mar. 15	Apr. 10–May 15.
Cucumber	Feb. 15–Mar. 15	Feb. 15–Apr. 15	Feb. 15–Apr. 15	Feb. 1–Mar. 15	Feb. 15–Apr. 15	Apr. 1–May 1	Apr. 15–May 15.
Eggplant[1]	Feb. 1–Mar. 1	Feb. 10–Mar. 15	Feb. 20–Apr. 1	Mar. 10–Apr. 15	Mar. 15–Apr. 15	Apr. 1–May 1	May 10–June 15.
Endive	Jan. 1–Mar. 1	Jan. 1–Mar. 1	Jan. 1–Mar. 1	Jan. 15–Mar. 1	Feb. 15–Mar. 15	Mar. 1–Apr. 1	Mar. 10–Apr. 10.
Fennel, Florence	Jan. 1–Mar. 1	Jan. 1–Mar. 1	Jan. 15–Mar. 1	Feb. 1–Mar. 1	Feb. 15–Mar. 15	Mar. 1–Apr. 1	Feb. 10–Mar. 10.
Garlic	(²)	(²)	Jan. 15–Mar. 15	Feb. 1–Mar. 1	Feb. 15–Mar. 15	Feb. 1–Mar. 1	Feb. 10–Mar. 10.
Horseradish[1]				(²)	(²)	(²)	Feb. 10–Mar. 10.
Kale	Jan. 1–Feb. 1	Jan. 10–Feb. 1	Jan. 20–Feb. 10	Feb. 1–20	Feb. 10–Mar. 1	Feb. 20–Mar. 10	Mar. 1–20.
Kohlrabi	Jan. 1–Feb. 1	Jan. 1–Feb. 1	Jan. 20–Feb. 10	Feb. 1–20	Feb. 10–Mar. 1	Feb. 15–Mar. 1	Mar. 1–Apr. 1.
Leek	Jan. 1–Feb. 1	Jan. 1–Feb. 1	Jan. 1–Feb. 1	Jan. 15–Feb. 15	Jan. 25–Mar. 1	Feb. 1–Mar. 1	Feb. 15–Mar. 15.
Lettuce, head[1]	Jan. 1–Feb. 1	Jan. 1–Feb. 1	Jan. 1–Mar. 15	Jan. 1–Mar. 15	Jan. 15–Apr. 15	Feb. 1–Apr. 1	Mar. 1–20.
Lettuce, leaf	Feb. 15–Mar. 15	Feb. 15–Apr. 15	Jan. 1–Mar. 15	Jan. 1–Mar. 15	Jan. 15–Apr. 15	Feb. 1–Apr. 1	Apr. 10–May 15.
Muskmelon	Feb. 15–Apr. 1	Feb. 15–Apr. 15	Feb. 15–Apr. 15	Feb. 1–Mar. 15	Feb. 10–Mar. 15	Feb. 20–Apr. 1	Apr. 10–May 15.
Mustard	Jan. 1–Mar. 1	Jan. 1–Mar. 1	Jan. 1–Mar. 1	Jan. 1–June 1	Mar. 20–June 1	Apr. 20–Apr. 1	Apr. 10–June 15.
Okra	Feb. 15–Apr. 1	Feb. 15–Apr. 1	Mar. 1–June 1	Mar. 10–June 1	Mar. 20–June 1	Apr. 10–June 1	Feb. 20–Apr. 15.
Onion[1]	Jan. 1–15	Jan. 1–15	Jan. 1–15	Jan. 1–Feb. 15	Jan. 1–Feb. 15	Jan. 1–Feb. 15	May 10–June 15.
Onion, seed	Jan. 1–15	Jan. 1–15	Jan. 1–15	Jan. 1–Feb. 15	Jan. 1–Mar. 1	Feb. 10–Mar. 10	Feb. 20–Mar. 15.
Onion, sets	Jan. 1–15	Jan. 1–15	Jan. 1–15	Jan. 1–Feb. 15	Jan. 15–Mar. 10	Feb. 1–Mar. 10	Feb. 20–Mar. 20.
Parsley	Jan. 1–30	Jan. 1–30	Jan. 1–30	Jan. 1–Feb. 1	Jan. 15–Mar. 10	Feb. 15–Mar. 20	Mar. 1–Apr. 1.
Parsnip				Jan. 1–Feb. 1	Jan. 15–Mar. 1	Feb. 15–Mar. 15	Mar. 1–Apr. 1.
Peas, garden	Jan. 1–Feb. 15	Jan. 1–Feb. 15	Jan. 1–Feb. 15	Jan. 1–Mar. 1	Jan. 15–Mar. 1	Feb. 1–Mar. 15	Mar. 1–20.
Peas, black-eye	Feb. 15–May 1	Feb. 15–May 15	Mar. 1–June 15	Mar. 10–June 20	Mar. 10–June 1	Mar. 10–Mar. 20	Feb. 10–Mar. 20.
Pepper[1]	Feb. 1–Apr. 1	Feb. 15–Apr. 15	Mar. 1–May 1	Mar. 15–May 1	Apr. 1–June 1	Apr. 15–July 1	Apr. 15–July 1.
Potato	Jan. 1–Feb. 15	Jan. 1–Feb. 15	Jan. 15–Mar. 1	Jan. 15–May 20	Feb. 1–Mar. 1	Feb. 10–Mar. 15	Apr. 15–June 1.
Radish	Jan. 1–Apr. 1	Jan. 1–Apr. 1	Jan. 1–Apr. 1	Jan. 1–Apr. 1	Jan. 1–Apr. 1	Jan. 20–May 1	Feb. 20–Mar. 20.
Rhubarb[1]							Feb. 20–Mar. 20.
Rutabaga	Jan. 1–Feb. 1	Jan. 1–Feb. 10	Jan. 15–Feb. 20	Jan. 1–Feb. 1	Jan. 15–Feb. 15	Feb. 1–Mar. 1	Feb. 1–Mar. 1.
Salsify	Jan. 1–Feb. 1	Jan. 1–Feb. 1	Jan. 15–Feb. 20	Jan. 15–Mar. 1	Feb. 1–Mar. 1	Feb. 15–Mar. 1	Feb. 1–Mar. 1.
Shallot	Jan. 1–Mar. 1	Jan. 1–Mar. 1	Jan. 15–Mar. 15	Jan. 15–Mar. 1	Jan. 15–Mar. 15	Feb. 15–Mar. 15	Mar. 1–20.
Sorrel	Jan. 1–Mar. 1	Jan. 1–Mar. 1	Jan. 15–Mar. 15	Feb. 1–Mar. 10	Feb. 10–Mar. 15	Feb. 20–Apr. 1	Mar. 1–15.
Soybean	Mar. 1–June 30	Mar. 1–June 30	Mar. 20–June 30	Mar. 20–June 30	Apr. 10–June 30	Apr. 10–June 30	Feb. 15–Mar. 15.
Spinach	Jan. 1–Feb. 15	Jan. 1–Feb. 15	Jan. 1–Mar. 1	Jan. 1–Mar. 1	Jan. 15–Mar. 1	Jan. 15–Mar. 15	Feb. 20–Apr. 1.
Spinach, New Zealand	Feb. 1–Apr. 15	Feb. 1–Apr. 15	Feb. 1–Apr. 15	Mar. 1–Apr. 15	Mar. 15–May 15	Apr. 1–May 15	Apr. 20–June 30.
Squash, summer	Feb. 15–Apr. 15	Feb. 15–Apr. 15	Feb. 15–Apr. 15	Mar. 1–May 15	Mar. 15–May 1	Apr. 1–May 15	Apr. 10–June 1.
Sweetpotato	Feb. 15–May 15	Feb. 15–May 15	Mar. 20–June 1	Mar. 20–June 1	Apr. 10–June 1	Apr. 10–May 20	Apr. 10–June 1.
Tomato	Feb. 1–Mar. 1	Feb. 20–Apr. 10	Feb. 20–Apr. 20	Mar. 1–Apr. 20	Mar. 20–May 10	Apr. 1–May 20	Apr. 10–June 1.
Turnip	Jan. 1–Mar. 1	Jan. 1–Mar. 1	Jan. 10–Mar. 1	Jan. 20–Mar. 1	Feb. 1–Mar. 1	Feb. 10–Mar. 10	Apr. 20–June 1.
Watermelon	Feb. 15–Mar. 15	Feb. 15–Apr. 1	Feb. 15–Apr. 15	Mar. 1–Apr. 15	Mar. 15–Apr. 15	Feb. 1–May 1	Apr. 10–May 15.

[1] Plants.

[2] Generally fall-planted (Table 2B).

See page 48 for instructions for using Tables and Maps.

TABLE 2A.—Earliest dates, and range of dates, for safe spring planting of vegetables in the open—Continued

Planting dates for localities in which average date of last freeze is—

Crop	Apr. 10	Apr. 20	Apr. 30	May 10	May 20	May 30	June 10
Asparagus[1]	Mar. 10–Apr. 10	Mar. 15–Apr. 15	Mar. 20–Apr. 15	Mar. 10–Apr. 30	Apr. 20–May 15	May 1–June 1	May 15–June 1.
Beans, lima	Apr. 1–June 30	May 1–June 20	May 15–June 15	May 25–June 15			
Beans, snap	Apr. 10–June 30	Apr. 25–June 30	May 10–June 30	May 10–June 30	May 15–June 30	May 25–June 15	May 15–June 15.
Beet	Mar. 10–June 1	Mar. 20–June 15	Apr. 10–June 30	May 1–June 15	May 1–June 15	May 10–June 10	May 20–June 10.
Broccoli, sprouting[1]	Mar. 15–Apr. 15	Mar. 25–Apr. 20	Apr. 1–June 15	May 1–June 15	May 1–June 15	May 10–June 10	May 20–June 10.
Brussels sprouts[1]	Mar. 15–Apr. 15	Mar. 25–Apr. 20	Apr. 1–May 1	Apr. 15–June 1	May 1–June 15	May 10–June 10	May 20–June 1.
Cabbage[1]	Mar. 1–Apr. 1	Mar. 10–Apr. 1	Apr. 15–May 15	Apr. 20–June 1	May 1–June 15	May 10–June 15	May 20–June 1.
Cabbage, Chinese	(²)	(²)	Apr. 10–May 1	Apr. 20–May 15	May 1–June 15	May 10–June 15	May 20–June 1.
Carrot	Mar. 10–Apr. 20	Apr. 1–May 15	Apr. 10–June 1	Apr. 20–June 15	May 15–June 15	May 20–June 1	June 1–June 15.
Cauliflower[1]	Mar. 1–Mar. 20	Mar. 15–Apr. 20	Apr. 10–May 10	Apr. 15–May 15	May 10–June 15	May 20–June 1	June 1–June 15.
Celery and celeriac	Apr. 1–Apr. 20	Apr. 10–May 10	Apr. 15–May 1	Apr. 20–June 15	May 10–June 15	May 20–June 1	June 1–June 15.
Chard	Mar. 15–June 15	Mar. 20–June 15	Apr. 20–June 15	May 1–June 15	May 10–June 15	May 20–June 1	May 15–May 15.
Chervil and chives	Mar. 1–Apr. 1	Mar. 10–Apr. 10	Apr. 10–May 10	Apr. 20–May 10	May 1–June 1	May 1–June 1	June 1–15.
Chicory, witloof	June 10–July 1	June 15–July 1	June 15–July 1	June 1–20	June 1–15	June 1–15	
Collards[1]	Mar. 1–June 1	Mar. 10–June 1	Apr. 1–June 1	Apr. 15–June 1	Apr. 15–June 1	May 1–June 15	May 15–June 15.
Cornsalad	Feb. 1–Apr. 1	Feb. 15–Apr. 15	Feb. 1–Apr. 1	Apr. 15–June 1	Apr. 15–June 1	May 10–June 1	May 15–June 1.
Cress, upland	Mar. 10–Apr. 15	Mar. 10–Apr. 15	Mar. 20–May 1	Apr. 10–June 1	Apr. 15–June 1	May 10–June 1	May 15–June 1.
Corn, sweet	Apr. 10–June 1	Apr. 25–June 15	May 10–June 15	May 10–June 15	May 15–June 1	May 20–June 1	
Cucumber	Apr. 20–June 1	May 1–June 15	May 15–June 15	May 20–June 15			
Eggplant[1]	May 1–June 1	May 10–June 15	May 15–June 10	June 1–15	June 1–15		
Endive	Mar. 15–Apr. 15	Mar. 25–Apr. 15	Apr. 1–May 1	Apr. 15–May 15	May 1–30	May 1–30	May 15–June 1.
Fennel, Florence	Mar. 15–Apr. 15	Mar. 25–Apr. 15	Apr. 1–May 1	Apr. 15–May 15	May 1–30	May 1–30	May 15–June 1.
Garlic	Feb. 20–Mar. 20	Mar. 10–Apr. 1	Mar. 15–Apr. 15	Apr. 1–May 1	Apr. 15–May 15	May 1–30	May 15–June 1.
Horseradish[1]	Mar. 10–Apr. 10	Mar. 10–Apr. 10	Apr. 1–30	Apr. 15–May 15	Apr. 20–May 20	May 1–30	May 15–June 1.
Kale	Mar. 10–Apr. 1	Mar. 20–Apr. 10	Apr. 1–20	Apr. 10–May 1	Apr. 20–May 10	May 1–30	May 15–June 1.
Kohlrabi	Mar. 10–Apr. 10	Mar. 20–May 1	Apr. 10–May 1	Apr. 15–May 15	Apr. 20–May 20	May 1–30	May 15–June 1.
Leek	Mar. 1–Apr. 1	Mar. 15–Apr. 15	Apr. 1–May 1	Apr. 15–June 1	May 1–May 20	May 1–June 1	1–15.
Lettuce, head[1]	Mar. 10–Apr. 1	Mar. 15–Apr. 15	Apr. 1–May 1	Apr. 15–May 15	May 1–June 30	May 10–June 30	May 20–June 30.
Lettuce, leaf	Mar. 15–May 15	Mar. 20–May 15	Apr. 1–June 1	Apr. 15–June 15	May 1–June 30	May 10–June 30	May 20–June 30.
Muskmelon	Apr. 20–June 1	May 1–June 15	May 15–June 15	May 20–June 15			
Mustard	Mar. 10–Apr. 20	Mar. 20–May 1	Apr. 10–June 1	Apr. 15–June 1	May 1–June 30	May 10–June 30	May 20–June 30.
Okra	Apr. 20–June 15	May 1–June 1	May 10–June 1	June 1–20	June 1–20		
Onion[1]	Mar. 1–Apr. 1	Mar. 15–Apr. 10	Apr. 1–May 1	Apr. 10–May 1	Apr. 20–May 15	May 1–30	May 10–June 10.
Onion, seed	Mar. 1–Apr. 1	Mar. 15–Apr. 1	Apr. 1–May 1	Apr. 1–May 1	Apr. 20–May 15	May 1–30	May 10–June 10.
Onion, sets	Mar. 1–Apr. 1	Mar. 15–Apr. 1	Apr. 1–May 1	Apr. 1–May 1	Apr. 15–May 10	May 1–30	May 10–June 10.
Parsley	Mar. 10–Apr. 10	Mar. 20–May 1	Apr. 1–May 1	Apr. 15–May 15	May 1–20	May 1–20	May 20–June 10.
Parsnip	Feb. 20–Mar. 20	Mar. 10–Apr. 10	Mar. 20–May 1	Apr. 15–June 1	May 1–20	May 1–20	May 10–June 10.
Peas, garden	May 1–July 1	May 1–June 1	Mar. 20–May 1	Apr. 15–June 1	Apr. 15–July 1	May 1–June 15	May 1–June 15.
Peas, black-eye	May 1–June 20	May 10–June 15	May 15–June 15	June 1–15			
Pepper[1]	May 1–June 1	May 10–June 1	May 15–June 10	June 1–15			
Potato	Mar. 10–Apr. 1	Mar. 20–May 10	Apr. 1–June 1	Apr. 15–June 15	May 1–June 15	June 1–June 15	June 15.
Radish	Mar. 1–May 1	Mar. 10–May 10	Apr. 1–June 1	Apr. 15–June 15	May 1–June 15	June 1–July 1	June 1–July 15.
Rhubarb[1]	Mar. 1–Apr. 1	Mar. 10–Apr. 10	Apr. 1–May 1	Apr. 15–May 10	Apr. 20–May 20	May 1–20	May 15–June 1.
Rutabaga			June 1	June 15	June 15		
Salsify	Mar. 10–Apr. 15	Mar. 20–May 1	Apr. 15–June 1	May 15–June 15	May 15–June 1	June 1–15	May 15–June 1.
Shallot	Mar. 1–Apr. 15	Mar. 15–May 15	Apr. 1–June 1	Apr. 1–June 1	Apr. 10–June 1	May 1–June 1	May 1–June 1.
Sorrel	Mar. 1–Apr. 15	Mar. 15–May 1	Apr. 15–June 1	Apr. 15–June 15	May 1–June 1	May 1–20	May 10–June 10.
Soybean	May 1–June 30	May 15–June 30	May 25–June 10	June 10			
Spinach	Feb. 15–Apr. 1	Mar. 1–Apr. 15	Mar. 20–Apr. 20	Apr. 1–June 15	Apr. 10–June 15	Apr. 20–June 15	May 1–June 15.
Spinach, New Zealand	Apr. 20–June 1	May 1–June 15	May 1–June 15	May 10–June 15	May 20–June 15	June 1–20	June 1–20.
Squash, summer	Apr. 20–June 1	May 1–June 15	May 1–30	June 10–20			June 15–20.
Sweetpotato	May 1–June 1	May 10–June 10	May 20–June 10				
Tomato	Mar. 1–Apr. 1	Mar. 20–May 10	Apr. 10–June 1	May 5–20	May 25–June 15	June 5–20	June 15–June 15.
Turnip	Mar. 1–Apr. 1	Mar. 10–Apr. 1	Mar. 20–May 1	Apr. 1–June 1	Apr. 15–June 1	May 1–June 15	May 1–June 15.
Watermelon	Apr. 20–June 1	May 1–June 15	May 15–June 15	May 20–May 10	June 15–July 1	May 1–June 15	May 15–June 15.

[1] Plants.

[2] Generally fall-planted (Table 2B).

See page 48 for instructions for using Tables and Maps.

TABLE 2B.—*Latest dates, and range of dates, for safe fall planting of vegetables in the open*

Crop	Planting dates for localities in which average dates of first freeze is—					
	Aug. 30	Sept. 10	Sept. 20	Sept. 30	Oct. 10	Oct. 20
Asparagus [1]					Oct. 20–Nov. 15	Nov. 1–Dec. 15.
Beans, lima				June 1–15	June 1–15	June 15–30.
Beans, snap		May 15–June 15	June 1–July 1	June 1–July 10	June 15–July 20	July 1–Aug. 1.
Beet	May 15–June 15	May 15–June 15	June 1–July 1	June 1–July 10	June 15–July 25	July 1–Aug. 5.
Broccoli, sprouting	May 1–June 1	May 1–June 1	May 1–June 15	June 1–30	June 15–July 15	July 1–Aug. 1.
Brussels sprouts	May 1–June 1	May 1–June 1	May 1–June 15	June 1–30	June 15–July 15	July 1–Aug. 1.
Cabbage [1]	May 1–June 1	May 1–June 1	May 1–June 15	June 1–July 10	June 1–July 15	July 1–20.
Cabbage, Chinese	May 15–June 15	May 15–June 15	June 1–July 1	June 1–July 15	June 15–Aug. 1	July 15–Aug. 15.
Carrot	May 15–June 15	May 15–June 15	June 1–July 1	June 1–July 10	June 1–July 20	June 15–Aug. 1.
Cauliflower [1]	May 1–June 1	May 1–July 1	May 1–July 1	May 10–July 15	June 1–July 25	July 1–Aug. 5.
Celery [1] and celeriac	May 1–June 1	May 15–June 15	May 15–July 1	June 1–July 5	June 1–July 15	June 1–Aug. 1.
Chard	May 15–June 15	May 15–July 1	June 1–July 1	June 1–July 5	June 1–July 20	June 1–Aug. 1.
Chervil and chives	May 10–June 10	May 1–June 15	May 15–June 15	(2)	(2)	(2)
Chicory, witloof	May 15–June 15	May 15–June 15	May 15–June 15	June 1–July 1	June 1–July 1	June 15–July 15.
Collards [1]	May 15–June 15	May 15–June 15	May 15–June 15	June 15–July 15	July 1–Aug. 1	July 15–Aug. 15.
Cornsalad	May 15–June 15	May 15–July 1	June 15–Aug. 1	July 15–Sept. 1	Aug. 15–Sept. 15	Sept. 1–Oct. 15.
Corn, sweet			June 1–July 1	June 1–July 1	June 1–July 10	June 1–July 20.
Cress, upland	May 15–June 15	May 15–July 1	June 15–Aug. 1	July 15–Sept. 1	Aug. 15–Sept. 15	Sept. 1–Oct. 15.
Cucumber			June 1–15	June 1–July 1	June 1–July 1	June 1–July 15.
Eggplant [1]				May 20–June 10	May 15–June 15	June 1–July 1.
Endive	June 1–July 1	June 1–July 1	June 15–July 15	June 15–Aug. 1	July 1–Aug. 15	July 15–Sept. 1.
Fennel, Florence	May 15–June 15	May 15–July 15	June 1–July 1	June 1–July 15	June 15–July 15	June 15–Aug. 1.
Garlic	(2)	(2)	(2)	(2)	(2)	(2)
Horseradish [1]	(2)	(2)	(2)	(2)	(2)	(2)
Kale	May 15–June 15	May 15–June 15	June 1–July 1	June 15–July 15	July 1–Aug. 1	July 15–Aug. 15.
Kohlrabi	May 15–June 15	June 1–July 1	June 1–July 15	June 15–July 15	July 1–Aug. 1	July 15–Aug. 15.
Leek	May 1–June 1	May 1–June 1	(2)	(2)	(2)	(2)
Lettuce, head [1]	May 15–July 1	May 15–July 15	June 1–July 15	June 15–Aug. 1	July 15–Aug. 15	Aug. 1–30.
Lettuce, leaf	May 15–July 15	May 15–July 15	June 1–Aug. 1	June 1–Aug. 1	July 15–Sept. 1	July 15–Sept. 1.
Muskmelon			May 1–June 15	May 15–June 1	June 1–June 15	June 15–July 20.
Mustard	May 15–July 15	May 15–July 15	June 1–Aug. 1	June 15–Aug. 1	July 15–Aug. 15	Aug. 1–Sept. 1.
Okra			June 1–20	June 1–July 1	June 1–July 15	June 1–Aug. 1.
Onion [1]	May 1–June 10	May 1–June 10	(2)	(2)	(2)	(2)
Onion, seed	May 1–June 1	May 1–June 10	(2)	(2)	(2)	(2)
Onion, sets	May 1–June 1	May 1–June 10	(2)	(2)	(2)	(2)
Parsley	May 15–June 15	May 15–June 15	June 1–July 1	June 1–July 15	June 15–Aug. 1	July 15–Aug. 15.
Parsnip	May 15–June 1	May 1–June 15	May 15–June 15	June 1–July 1	June 1–July 10	(2)
Peas, garden	May 10–June 15	May 1–July 1	June 1–July 15	June 1–Aug. 1	(2)	(2)
Peas, black-eye					June 1–July 1	June 1–July 1.
Pepper [1]			June 1–June 20	June 1–July 1	June 1–July 1	June 1–July 10.
Potato	May 15–June 1	May 1–June 15	May 1–June 15	May 1–June 15	May 15–June 15	June 15–July 15.
Radish	May 1–July 15	May 1–Aug. 1	June 1–Aug. 15	July 1–Sept. 1	July 15–Sept. 15	Aug. 1–Oct. 1.
Rhubarb [1]	Sept. 1–Oct. 1	Sept. 15–Oct. 15	Sept. 15–Nov. 1	Oct. 1–Nov. 1	Oct. 15–Nov. 15	Oct. 15–Dec. 1.
Rutabaga	May 15–June 15	May 1–June 15	June 1–July 1	June 1–July 1	June 1–July 15	July 10–20.
Salsify	May 15–June 1	May 10–June 10	May 20–June 20	June 1–20	June 1–July 1	June 1–July 1.
Shallot	(2)	(2)	(2)	(2)	(2)	(2)
Sorrel	May 15–June 15	May 1–June 15	June 1–July 1	June 1–July 15	July 1–Aug. 1	July 15–Aug. 15.
Soybean				May 25–June 10	June 1–25	June 1–July 5.
Spinach	May 15–July 1	June 1–July 15	June 1–Aug. 1	July 1–Aug. 15	Aug. 1–Sept. 1	Aug. 20–Sept. 10.
Spinach, New Zealand				May 15–July 1	June 1–July 15	June 1–Aug. 1.
Squash, summer	June 10–20	June 1–20	May 15–July 1	June 1–July 1	June 1–July 15	June 1–July 20.
Squash, winter			May 20–June 10	June 1–15	June 1–July 1	June 1–July 1.
Sweetpotato					May 20–June 10	June 1–15.
Tomato	June 20–30	June 10–20	June 1–20	June 1–20	June 1–20	June 1–July 1.
Turnip	May 15–June 15	June 1–July 1	June 1–July 15	June 1–Aug. 1	July 1–Aug. 1	July 15–Aug. 15.
Watermelon			May 1–June 15	May 15–June 1	June 1–June 15	June 15–July 20.

[1] Plants.

[2] Generally spring-planted (Table 2A).

See page 48 for instructions for using Tables and Maps.

Crop	Planting dates for localities in which average date of first freeze is—					
	Oct. 30	Nov. 10	Nov. 20	Nov. 30	Dec. 10	Dec. 20
Asparagus [1]	Nov. 15–Jan. 1	Dec. 1–Jan. 1				
Beans, lima	July 1–Aug. 1	July 1–Aug. 15	July 15–Sept. 1	Aug. 1–Sept. 15	Sept. 1–30	Sept. 1–Oct. 1.
Beans, snap	July 1–Aug. 15	July 1–Sept. 1	July 1–Sept. 10	Aug. 15–Sept. 20	Sept. 1–30	Sept. 1–Nov. 1.
Beet	Aug. 1–Sept. 1	Aug. 1–Oct. 1	Sept. 1–Dec. 1	Sept. 1–Dec. 15	Sept. 1–Dec. 31	Sept. 1–Dec. 31.
Broccoli, sprouting	July 1–Aug. 15	Aug. 1–Sept. 1	Aug. 1–Sept. 15	Aug. 1–Oct. 1	Aug. 1–Nov. 1	Sept. 1–Dec. 31.
Brussels sprouts	July 1–Aug. 15	Aug. 1–Sept. 1	Aug. 1–Sept. 15	Aug. 1–Oct. 1	Aug. 1–Nov. 1	Sept. 1–Dec. 31.
Cabbage [1]	Aug. 1–Sept. 1	Sept. 1–15	Sept. 1–Dec. 1	Sept. 1–Dec. 31	Sept. 1–Dec. 31	Sept. 1–Dec. 31.
Cabbage, Chinese	Aug. 1–Sept. 15	Aug. 15–Oct. 1	Sept. 1–Dec. 1	Sept. 1–Nov. 1	Sept. 1–Nov. 15	Sept. 1–Dec. 1.
Carrot	July 1–Aug. 15	Aug. 1–Sept. 1	Sept. 1–Nov. 1	Sept. 15–Dec. 1	Sept. 15–Dec. 1	Sept. 15–Dec. 1.
Cauliflower [1]	July 15–Aug. 15	Aug. 1–Sept. 1	Aug. 1–Sept. 15	Aug. 15–Oct. 10	Sept. 1–Oct. 20	Sept. 15–Nov. 1.
Celery [1] and celeriac	June 15–Aug. 15	July 1–Aug. 15	July 15–Sept. 1	Aug. 1–Dec. 1	Sept. 1–Dec. 31	Oct. 1–Dec. 31.
Chard	June 1–Sept. 10	June 1–Sept. 15	June 1–Oct. 1	June 1–Nov. 1	June 1–Dec. 1	June 1–Dec. 31.
Chervil and chives	(2)	(2)	Nov. 1–Dec. 31	Nov. 1–Dec. 31	Nov. 1–Dec. 31	Nov. 1–Dec. 31.
Chicory, witloof	July 1–Aug. 10	July 10–Aug. 20	July 20–Sept. 1	Aug. 15–Sept. 30	Aug. 15–Oct. 15	Aug. 15–Oct. 15.
Collards [1]	Aug. 1–Sept. 15	Aug. 1–Sept. 15	Aug. 25–Nov. 1	Sept. 1–Dec. 1	Sept. 1–Dec. 31	Sept. 1–Dec. 31.
Cornsalad	Sept. 15–Nov. 1	Oct. 1–Dec. 1	Oct. 1–Dec. 1	Oct. 1–Dec. 31	Oct. 1–Dec. 31	Oct. 1–Dec. 31.
Corn, sweet	June 1–Aug. 1	June 1–Aug. 15	June 1–Sept. 1			
Cress, upland	Sept. 15–Nov. 1	Oct. 1–Dec. 1	Oct. 1–Dec. 1	Oct. 1–Dec. 31	Oct. 1–Dec. 1	Oct. 1–Dec. 31.
Cucumber	June 1–Aug. 1	June 1–Aug. 15	June 1–Aug. 15	July 15–Sept. 15	Aug. 15–Oct. 1	Aug. 15–Oct. 1.
Eggplant [1]	June 1–July 1	June 1–July 15	June 1–Aug. 1	July 1–Sept. 1	Aug. 1–Sept. 30	Aug. 1–Sept. 30.
Endive	July 15–Aug. 15	Aug. 1–Sept. 1	Sept. 1–Oct. 1	Sept. 1–Nov. 15	Sept. 1–Dec. 31	Sept. 1–Dec. 31.
Fennel, Florence	July 1–Aug. 1	July 15–Aug. 15	Aug. 15–Sept. 15	Sept. 1–Nov. 15	Sept. 1–Dec. 1	Sept. 1–Dec. 1.
Garlic	(2)	Aug. 1–Oct. 1	Aug. 15–Oct. 1	Sept. 1–Nov. 15	Sept. 15–Nov. 15	Sept. 15–Nov. 15.
Horseradish [1]	(2)	(2)	(2)	(2)	(2)	(2)
Kale	July 15–Sept. 1	Aug. 1–Sept. 15	Aug. 15–Oct. 15	Sept. 1–Dec. 1	Sept. 1–Dec. 31	Sept. 1–Dec. 31.
Kohlrabi	Aug. 1–Sept. 1	Aug. 15–Sept. 15	Sept. 1–Oct. 15	Sept. 1–Dec. 1	Sept. 15–Dec. 31	Sept. 1–Dec. 31.
Leek	(2)	(2)	Sept. 1–Nov. 1	Sept. 1–Nov. 1	Sept. 1–Nov. 1	Sept. 15–Nov. 1
Lettuce, head [1]	Aug. 1–Sept. 15	Aug. 15–Oct. 15	Sept. 1–Nov. 1	Sept. 1–Dec. 1	Sept. 15–Dec. 31	Sept. 15–Dec. 31.
Lettuce, leaf	Aug. 15–Oct. 1	Aug. 25–Oct. 1	Sept. 1–Nov. 1	Sept. 1–Dec. 1	Sept. 15–Dec. 31	Sept. 15–Dec. 31.
Muskmelon	July 1–July 15	July 15–July 30				Sept. 15–Dec. 1.
Mustard	Aug. 15–Oct. 15	Aug. 15–Nov. 1	Sept. 1–Dec. 1	Sept. 1–Dec. 1	Sept. 1–Dec. 31	Sept. 1–Dec. 31.
Okra	June 1–Aug. 10	June 1–Aug. 20	June 1–Sept. 10	June 1–Sept. 20	Aug. 1–Oct. 1	Aug. 1–Oct. 1.
Onion [1]		Sept. 1–Oct. 15	Oct. 1–Dec. 31	Oct. 1–Dec. 31	Oct. 1–Dec. 31	Oct. 1–Dec. 31.
Onion, seed			Sept. 1–Nov. 1	Sept. 1–Nov. 1	Sept. 1–Nov. 1	Sept. 15–Nov. 1.
Onion, sets		Oct. 1–Dec. 1	Nov. 1–Dec. 31	Nov. 1–Dec. 31	Nov. 1–Dec. 31	Nov. 1–Dec. 31.
Parsley	Aug. 1–Sept. 15	Sept. 1–Nov. 15	Sept. 1–Dec. 31	Sept. 1–Dec. 31	Sept. 1–Dec. 31	Sept. 1–Dec. 31.
Parsnip	(2)	(2)	Aug. 1–Sept. 1	Sept. 1–Nov. 15	Sept. 1–Dec. 1	Sept. 1–Dec. 1.
Peas, garden	Aug. 1–Sept. 15	Sept. 1–Nov. 1	Oct. 1–Dec. 1	Oct. 1–Dec. 31	Oct. 1–Dec. 31	Oct. 1–Dec. 31.
Peas, black-eye	June 1–Aug. 1	June 15–Aug. 15	July 1–Sept. 1	July 1–Sept. 10	July 1–Sept. 20	July 1–Sept. 20.
Pepper [1]	June 1–July 20	June 1–Aug. 1	June 1–Aug. 15	June 15–Sept. 1	Aug. 15–Oct. 1	Aug. 15–Oct. 1.
Potato	July 20–Aug. 10	July 25–Aug. 20	Aug. 10–Sept. 15	Aug. 1–Sept. 15	Aug. 1–Sept. 15	Aug. 1–Sept. 15.
Radish	Aug. 15–Oct. 15	Sept. 1–Nov. 15	Sept. 1–Dec. 1	Sept. 1–Dec. 1	Aug. 1–Sept. 15	Oct. 1–Dec. 31.
Rhubarb [1]	Nov. 1–Dec. 1					
Rutabaga	July 15–Aug. 1	July 15–Aug. 15	Aug. 1–Sept. 1	Sept. 1–Nov. 15	Oct. 1–Nov. 15	Oct. 15–Nov. 15.
Salsify	June 1–July 10	June 15–July 20	July 15–Aug. 15	Aug. 15–Sept. 30	Aug. 15–Oct. 15	Sept. 1–Oct. 31.
Shallot	(2)	Aug. 1–Oct. 1	Aug. 15–Oct. 1	Aug. 15–Oct. 15	Sept. 15–Nov. 1	Sept. 15–Nov. 1.
Sorrel	Aug. 1–Sept. 15	Aug. 15–Oct. 1	Aug. 15–Oct. 15	Sept. 1–Nov. 15	Sept. 1–Dec. 15	Sept. 1–Dec. 31.
Soybean	June 1–July 15	June 1–July 25	June 1–July 30	June 1–July 30	June 1–July 30	June 1–July 30.
Spinach	Sept. 1–Oct. 1	Sept. 15–Nov. 1	Oct. 1–Dec. 1	Oct. 1–Dec. 31	Oct. 1–Dec. 31	Oct. 1–Dec. 31.
Spinach, New Zealand	June 1–Aug. 1	June 1–Aug. 15	June 1–Aug. 15			
Squash, summer	June 1–Aug. 1	June 1–Aug. 10	June 1–Aug. 20	June 1–Sept. 1	June 1–Sept. 15	June 1–Oct. 1.
Squash, winter	June 10–July 10	June 20–July 20	July 1–Aug. 1	July 15–Aug. 15	Aug. 1–Sept. 1	Aug. 1–Sept. 1.
Sweetpotato	June 1–15	June 1–July 1	June 1–July 1	June 1–July 1	June 1–July 1	June 1–July 1.
Tomato	June 1–Aug. 1	June 1–July 15	June 1–Aug. 15	Aug. 1–Sept. 1	Aug. 15–Oct. 1	Sept. 1–Nov. 1.
Turnip	Aug. 1–Sept. 15	Sept. 1–Oct. 15	Sept. 1–Nov. 15	Sept. 1–Nov. 15	Oct. 1–Dec. 1	Oct. 1–Dec. 31.
Watermelon	July 1–July 15	July 15–July 30				

[1] Plants.

[2] Generally spring-planted (Table 2A).

See page 48 for instructions for using Tables and Maps.

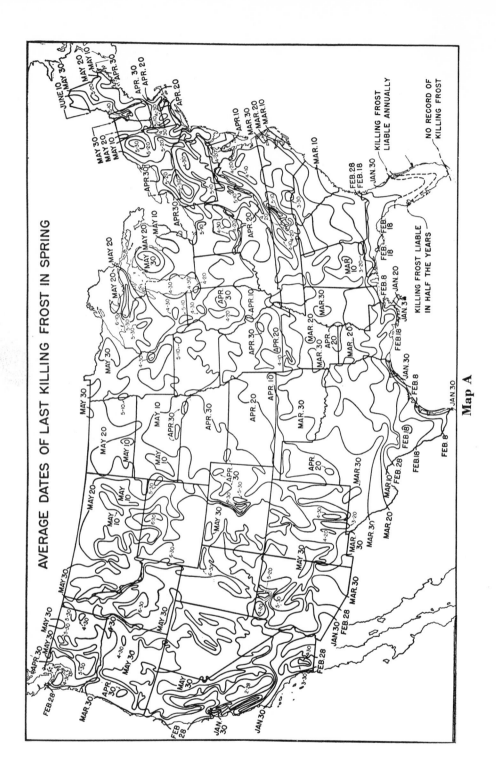

AVERAGE DATES OF LAST KILLING FROST IN SPRING

Map A

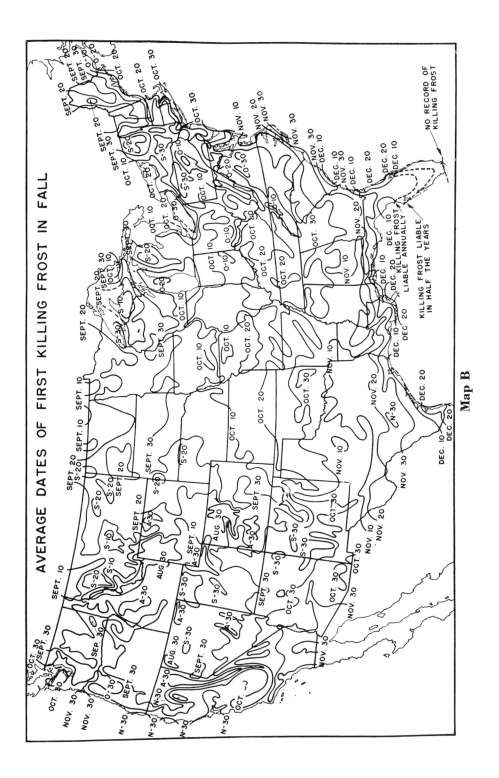

AVERAGE DATES OF FIRST KILLING FROST IN FALL

Map B

HOW TO USE FROST MAPS AND TABLES 2A AND 2B

Map A shows the average dates of the last killing frost in spring. Table 2A gives planting dates that not only indicate how early it is safe to plant, but also the spring and summer dates beyond which planting usually gives poor results.

The first date beside the vegetables listed in Table 2A denotes the earliest generally safe date that the crop can be sown or transplanted. The second date is the latest that a successful planting can be made.

To determine the best time to plant in the spring for your locality:

1. Find your area on Map A and the solid line that comes nearest to it.
2. Check the date on the solid line. It represents the average date of the last killing frost. The first number indicates the month; the second number, the day. Thus 5-10 is May 10. Once you know the date you no longer need the map.
3. Look at Table 2A, locate the column that has your date in it, and encircle the column. It is the only column you'll consult.
4. Ascertain the dates in the column that are on a line with the crop you plan to plant. These dates show the period during which it can be safely planted. Generally speaking, the best time is on, or soon after, the first of the two dates. A time midway between them is very good, the second date is apt to be too late.

To find the dates for late plantings use Map B—which shows the average dates of the first killing frosts in autumn—in conjunction with Table 2B.

familiarity with frost maps and planting tables, most gardeners have difficulty deciding when to plant. Some take a calculated risk and plant early. Others wait until they are sure frost is unlikely. The first group reasons that, if the weather cooperates, they will be able to reap two harvests—one in midsummer, the other in the fall. But the second group is convinced that extremely early planting is too risky because vegetables "come along" quickly in consistently warm weather.

But even when all danger of frost is past, an experienced gardener waits until the soil, saturated with moisture from melted snow, dries out before he plants. Not only do vegetables dislike "wet feet" but also water replaces air in the soil. As a result, roots suffocate from a lack of oxygen. Because gardens on slopes and those whose soil has a high sand content drain

TABLE 3

Approximate planting times for the tender and hardy
vegetables most commonly grown in backyard gardens

Cold hardy plants for early spring planting		Cold tender or heat hardy plants for later spring or early summer planting			Hardy plants for late summer or fall planting, except in North (plant 6–8 weeks before first fall freeze)
Very hardy (plant 4–6 weeks before frost-free date)	Hardy (plant 2–4 weeks before frost-free date)	Not cold hardy (plant on frost-free date)	Requiring hot weather (plant one week or more after frost-free date)	Medium heat tolerant (good for summer planting)	
Broccoli Cabbage Lettuce Onions Potatoes Spinach Turnip	Beets Carrots Chard Radish	Beans, snap New Zealand spinach Squash Sweet corn Tomato	Beans, lima Cucumbers Eggplant Melons Peppers	Beans, all Chard New Zealand spinach Squash Sweet corn	Beets Lettuce Spinach Turnip

quickly, they can usually be planted long before plots in depressions or clayey soil. Nevertheless, some gardeners whose soil takes considerable time to dry sow seed early. They plant in raised beds filled with synthetic soil. Directions for making raised beds and manufacturing soil substitutes are given in the chapter dealing with container gardening.

"Get seed in the ground as soon as the soil can be worked" is an old gardening rule. Certain authorities claim that one can tell whether or not to start planting by making a soil "snowball." They maintain that if the ball remains compacted when pressed gently with the thumb, the ground is too wet to plant. But if the ball crumbles readily, the moisture content of the soil is suitable for sowing seed. Obviously, the results of this test depend upon the type of soil molded into a ball and how much pressure is applied. A far more practical method of deciding whether the ground has dried out sufficiently is to walk across a garden. If soil sticks to your shoes, it is too wet to plant.

Preparing to Plant

Turning a garden over with a rotary tiller or other mechanical device is an easy task. Doing the job with a spading fork is hard work—particu-

1.

2.

3.

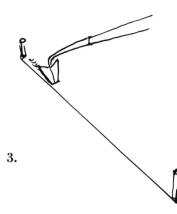

4.

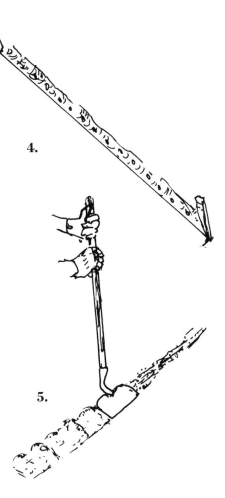

5.

Planting sequence:
1. Turn over garden soil, break clods, and apply fertilizer.
2. Rake the area smooth, removing stones and debris.
3. Lay out rows with aid of twine guide and make furrows for small seeds with the handle of a hoe, and furrows for large seeds with hoe blade.
4. Sow seeds and cover with soil.
5. Tamp row with back of hoe blade.

larly if a plot has not been tilled previously. Therefore don't attempt to dig up your garden all at once. If you do, the chances are that you'll find gardening a chore rather than a pleasure. Turn over your garden in stages and, if weather and soil conditions permit, plant a row or two as space becomes available. The fun of sowing seed will make the digging seem worthwhile.

While working a garden with a spading fork, thrust the tines full length into the soil and turn over approximately eight inches of topsoil. Overlap each forkful to insure that the entire area is spaded. Any roots uncovered should be cut with pruning shears or an old axe (soil ruins an axe's cutting edge) and then pulled out of the ground. To reclaim topsoil, either break up clods with a hoe or repeatedly toss them into the air and catch them on the fork—just as if you were flipping pancakes—until they are pulverized. After spading, rake the entire surface smooth and remove all debris and stones.

Sowing Seed Outdoors

Consult your garden plan before planting! Otherwise, you may make such easily avoided mistakes as sowing tall-growing vegetables where they will shade low crops or run rows in the wrong direction. Remember, rows extending north to south provide plants with maximum sunshine throughout the day. Of course, if your garden is on a slope, rows should be placed east and west to avoid erosion.

While commercial growers broadcast seeds, backyard gardeners usually sow them in rows (often called drills) or in "hills." The latter term is a misnomer. "Hills" are merely depressions in which corn and vine crops are sown. As the plants grow the depressions are filled in, and soil is mounded around the plants when they are cultivated.

When making rows use heavy twine tightly tied to planting sticks as a guide. Open up furrows for small seeds by drawing the handle of a hoe along the twine, make furrows for large seeds with the blade of the hoe in the same way. While certain seeds require deeper planting than others, generally speaking, all seeds should be sown at a depth equal to four times their diameter. However, like all rules, this one has exceptions. In wet

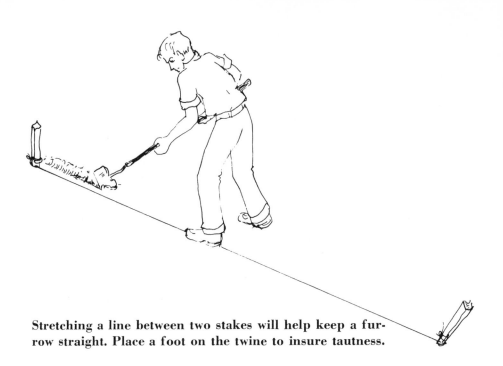

Stretching a line between two stakes will help keep a fur-row straight. Place a foot on the twine to insure tautness.

weather and in clayey soil, plant seeds shallower than directed on packets. Conversely, in dry spells or in light, sandy soil, sow seeds deeper than suggested.

Irrespective of weather or soil conditions, cover seeds with soil as soon as they are planted. Push the soil back into the furrow with a hoe and tamp it with the flat of a hoe, a short piece of two-by-four studding, or the palm of the hand.

Moisture is essential for seed germination. When sowing in dry weather, sprinkle plantings with a fine mist from a hose. Take special care when watering if your soil packs when wet. Seedlings may not be able to penetrate it if it becomes too compacted. You can help them break through caked soil by *gently* raking the surface of rows.

After firming and watering the soil, remove the guideline, then label the row. While seed packets supported by sturdy twigs can be used as labels, they often are blown away in high winds or reduced to matted globs of pulp by prolonged rains. The wooden labels available at garden centers are more satisfactory. Not only do they withstand exposure to the weather but also they provide space to record data that can be used when planning

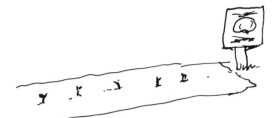

While seed packets supported by stakes can be used to mark rows, garden labels available at supply shops are more satisfactory as they do not disintegrate in rainy weather.

future gardens. If you write the variety of seed planted, where it was bought, and the planting date on the label with an indelible pencil, you can determine which varieties grow best in your garden.

There are several ways to sow seeds. One method is to tear a corner off the seed packet and tap the seeds into the ground. Another technique is to hold a pinch of seeds between the thumb and index finger and rub them together as one moves along a row. The best way to plant extremely small seeds is to mix them with white sand in a saltcellar and shake it over the furrow. The white sand will stand out against the soil and thus helps con-

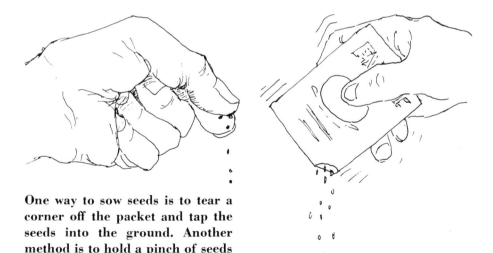

One way to sow seeds is to tear a corner off the packet and tap the seeds into the ground. Another method is to hold a pinch of seeds between the thumb and index finger and rub them together as one moves along a row.

All seeds should be sown at a depth equal to four times its diameter.

trol the spacing of tiny seeds that are hard to handle.

Still another planting method consists of dropping from two to six seeds at regular intervals along a row. This is an excellent way to sow in soil that crusts when it dries out after a rain. A single seedling may be unable to penetrate the crust—although a sprouting seed has considerable strength —but several will exert more than enough pressure to break the soil apart. Another advantage of group sowing is that it reduces the possibility of gaps due to poor germination. In all probability, some seeds in each group will sprout.

Seeds—particularly those that germinate slowly—can be aided in breaking through crusted soil by mixing them with radish seeds. Radish seedlings often appear within four days. As a result, they not only loosen crusted soil but also mark a row so that it can be weeded before the other seedlings emerge. If your soil compacts, but you don't like radishes, try this trick. Instead of covering seeds with soil, fill the furrows with a mixture of peat and sand. Seedlings will penetrate this combination without difficulty.

All vegetables demand a certain amount of room to have normal growth. The distance each requires is indicated on seed packets. While large seeds can be spaced when sown, there is no way of knowing the rate of germination or if their seedlings will establish themselves. This is be-

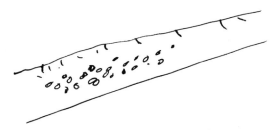

Sowing seeds too thickly is not only a waste, but also will make thinning plants a more difficult task.

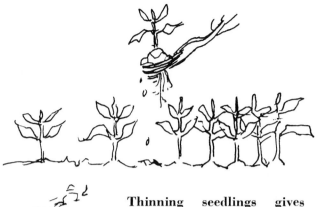

Thinning seedlings gives each plant the room it requires to grow and develop.

cause both seeds and seedlings are affected by soil conditions, temperature, planting depth, and moisture. The problem is to avoid overplanting—which wastes seed and makes thinning difficult—and still get an even stand of seedlings. However, most gardeners sow seed fairly thickly and then thin out seedlings before they crowd one another. Incidentally, with the exception of beets, lettuce, and members of the cabbage family, it is not practical to attempt to transplant seedlings thinned from rows.

Thinning, like hand weeding, is a tiresome chore. But it is an absolute necessity. Unless each plant has room to grow and develop, it becomes weak and spindly. Start thinning when seedlings are two to three inches tall by pulling out every other plant. Two weeks later, thin again. Although vegetables will thrive if their leaves merely touch those of another plant, they rarely do well if the leaves overlap. You may have to make as many as four thinnings to provide plants with sufficient room. But there is a bonus for thinning in midsummer—the beet greens, baby beets, and small, tender carrots removed from the rows.

Starting Seed Indoors

Residents of the warmer sections of the United States can sow the seeds of most vegetables in the open and reap a harvest. Elsewhere, the growing season is too short for cauliflower, eggplant, peppers, tomatoes, and other

Preplanted vegetable starter kits are available in supermarkets and garden supply shops. They make raising transplants very easy.

Seedlings reach transplant size quickly when subjected to a combination of natural and artificial light. Note the peat pots in the foreground.

A cut-down milk carton (left) with drainage holes pierced through its bottom makes an excellent "flat." Pellet (right) to transplant in three steps: plant seed in pellet, water, and let seedling grow until it is big enough to set outdoors. Peat pellets expand into "pots" when moistened. Plants raised in them suffer no transplanting shock.

tender vegetables to mature from seed. Where these crops cannot be sown directly in the garden, started plants must be set out after all danger of frost is past.

Started vegetable plants may be purchased from nurserymen, supermarkets, or garden supply centers. But it is much less expensive and far more fun to raise them yourself indoors. Growing vegetables from seed to transplant size also permits one to raise varieties that are not available locally.

However, don't make the mistake of sowing too many seeds indoors. In order for seedlings to make good growth they must be set a considerable distance apart in boxes or placed in individual pots as soon as they are big enough to handle. The young plants then have to receive from six to twelve hours of full sunshine daily. Thus it pays to check the number of sunny windows in your house before sowing seed indoors.

Practically any container that has drainage holes can be used to germinate seed and to start seedlings. Flats (topless wooden or plastic boxes) are the most popular containers. But the use of a series of cubes composed of plant-growing materials is increasing. Seed is sown in the cubes after they are thoroughly watered. Pellets fashioned from peat that expand into

The bottom of a gallon plastic jug can be used to start seeds, while the top section will protect transplants on cold nights.

"pots" when moistened are the favorite containers of many gardeners who formerly used pots molded from peat. Not only is very little space required to store pellets but also there is no need to fill them with soil. Both peat pots and pellets have one advantage over all other containers: plant roots have no difficulty penetrating their walls. As a result, vegetables raised in them do not have to be removed from them when set outdoors and therefore experience no transplanting shock.

Flats, pellets, and other fiber containers are relatively inexpensive. But homemade containers—which do not eliminate transplanting shock—cost nothing. You can fashion containers from berry boxes, the plastic tubs in which cottage cheese, margarine, and other products are sold, or cut-off milk cartons. Plastic jugs can also be used. They should be cut about three inches from the bottom, and the top sections should be saved to cover tender transplants on cold nights after they are placed outdoors. Be sure to punch drainage holes in all homemade containers.

Ideally, seed should always be sown in a disease-free medium. But it is almost impossible to insure that a garden contains no harmful organisms. On the other hand, the danger of seeds becoming infected can be elimi-

These cabbage plants growing in synthetic soil are almost ready to transplant.

nated when they are planted indoors. The starting mediums sold at garden supply shops—vermiculite (a form of mica), sphagnum moss, and synthetic soils—do not have to be sterilized but ordinary garden soil does. One method is to flood it with boiling water. Another way is to bake it in a shallow pan for forty-five minutes with the oven set at 350°. You can tell when the soil is "done" by inserting a medium-sized potato in it. When the potato is baked, the soil will be sterilized.

A combination of soil, sphagnum moss, and vermiculite makes an excellent plant-starting medium. Place approximately two inches of sterilized soil over the bottom of a container, then fill it almost to the top with moss and vermiculite. Seedlings grown in this mix will rarely die from "damping-off"—wilting caused by disease organisms.

Damping-off can also be prevented by sowing seed in containers containing only vermiculite. Before planting, dampen the vermiculite and, after the seed is sown and firmed down, water the vermiculite lightly. Vermiculite has one great advantage over all other mediums—seedlings can be removed from it with practically no damage to their roots. However, vermiculite contains no nutrients. Plants raised in it must be fed with

Unless soil is sterilized disease organisms may cause seedlings growing in containers to "damp off."

a water soluble fertilizer.

Containers holding germinating and growing mediums other than vermiculite must be thoroughly soaked after being filled. When all the excess water has drained away, mark out rows, scatter seed along them, cover and firm. To retain the moisture essential for germination, the containers should be covered with plastic bags. The danger of the plastic touching the growing medium and causing mold to form is easily avoided. Merely support the bags with wickets fashioned from fine wire.

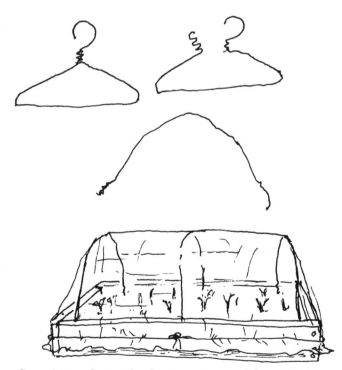

Covering a flat with plastic supported by wickets made from coat hangers transforms it into a greenhouse.

Portable coldframe constructed from pipe and plastic film. Note the flat of tomato plants in the right-hand corner of the frame.

A coldframe placed in front of a cellar window will receive some heat from a household heater.

While seeds can be germinated and seedlings "brought on" in flats, flowerpots, or other containers, a coldframe or a hotbed provides a more efficient method of starting vegetable plants. A coldframe consists of a rectangular box made of planks with a glass cover. The back of the box is

Hotbeds can be heated by an electric cable buried beneath the soil. Note the thermostat on the left-hand side of the backboard that controls the temperature in the frame.

raised so that the cover slants, permitting water to run off and the maximum amount of sunlight to reach plantings. Because coldframes are unheated they should be set in a shallow pit and banked with earth, sawdust, or other insulation. Burlap bags or carpeting thrown over the glass on cold nights give plants in a coldframe additional protection. But it is a waste of time, effort, and money to sow seeds in a coldframe early in the spring in cool or moderate regions. The soil is too cold for them to germinate. However, seedlings of such hardy vegetables as cabbage and lettuce can be placed in a coldframe long before the arrival of warm weather. Even a light frost will not damage them.

A hotbed is merely a coldframe furnished with heat by an electrical unit, steam, hot air, hot water from a nearby house, or by rotting manure. Heat-loving, tender plants thrive in hotbeds if they receive proper care. Hotbeds can also be used to grow lettuce, radishes, and other small crops during the winter months. But the ever-rising cost of all types of fuel makes heating a hotbed expensive. Then, too, a hotbed demands constant attention. On warm days the cover must be raised to provide ventilation and, if the weather suddenly changes, it has to be lowered quickly. As a result, hot-beds cannot be left unattended.

Transplanting

Lifting a plant and resetting it in other soil or putting it in a different place is called transplanting. All vegetables raised on windowsills or in coldframes, hotbeds, or greenhouses have to be transplanted at least twice. The first time, the seedlings are shifted from seedbeds to other containers. As indicated, this gives the young plants room to grow. While spacing seedlings two inches or more apart in flats will generally produce stocky plants, better growth results if seedlings are placed singly in pots, plant bands (nutrient impregnated bottomless fiber "pots"), or paper cups.

Don't be confused by the rule: "Transplant seedlings as soon as they are large enough to handle." All it means is that seedlings should be transplanted when they have developed two sets of true leaves. The soil into which they are transplanted will furnish ample food if it is enriched with a very small amount of commercial fertilizer.

Unless seedlings are removed from a starting medium carefully, their roots may be injured. Before lifting young plants from a container, give

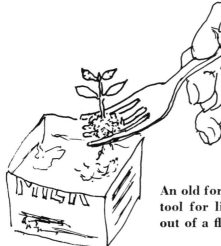

An old fork is the perfect tool for lifting seedlings out of a flat.

them a soaking. Then, using an old kitchen fork or a notched stick, *gently* prick out the seedlings with as much of the growing medium sticking to their roots as possible.

Because seedlings have extremely brittle stems, they are best handled by the leaves during transplanting. Even so, their growth will be temporarily checked. Watering with a soluble fertilizer will help them recover from transplanting shock. But fertilizer will not enable the plants to withstand the heat of the sun. Unless they are shaded for a day or two, they will wilt.

Sometimes it is necessary to shift large transplants into bigger containers or to reset them farther apart in flats. However, generally speaking, the second transplanting of vegetables consists of placing them in the ground. Before they are moved outdoors, the plants must be toughened. Otherwise, they may not adjust to their new environment. While a coldframe is the ideal place to "harden off" transplants, they can be conditioned to withstand cool weather and chilling winds by placing them in a sheltered spot for about two weeks, watering sparingly, and bringing them inside if frost is predicted. The lack of water and exposure to lower temperatures will slow the plants' growth and toughen them.

Cabbage transplants hardened off in a coldframe can be transplanted into the garden early in the spring.

A transplant, whether a bush, tree, or vegetable plant, should be placed in a depression that will hold water.

Cabbage, lettuce, and other hardy vegetables "harden off" quickly. Thus they can be planted in the open quite early. But peppers, tomatoes, and other tender vegetables cannot be toughened and should not be set outdoors until warm weather.

Special precautions must be taken to avoid harming the roots of flat-raised vegetables during transplanting. About a week before they are placed in the garden, cut the soil between each plant with a sharp knife, just as if you were blocking squares in a pan of fudge. This severing of the long tangled roots stimulates the growth of new roots which help the plants overcome transplanting shock. The new roots also bind the soil together, making it easier to lift plants out of a flat with a "root ball." Incidentally, an old fork makes an excellent tool for this purpose.

To get the largest possible root ball, try this gardening trick—water flats a few hours before you remove the plants growing in them. The water packs down the soil and, as a result, more of it adheres to the roots.

Although vegetable plants vary in their ability to withstand transplanting shock, losses can be reduced by following a few simple rules. One of the most important is to fill the holes in which transplants are to be set with water and let it soak into the soil before planting. Also be sure to sink transplants deeper than they stood in containers so that more of their stems are covered with soil. To prevent the drying out of the roots of vegetables

65

Being set in compost should help this transplant establish itself quickly. Note the large ball of soil around the roots.

in fibrous containers, place the "pots" well below the soil line.

After transplanting, pack the soil down around the plant—not too hard or you'll injure the tender roots—so that it is in the center of a depression that will catch water. Finally, water the transplant with plain water or with a starter solution. If you want to make your own solution rather than use a commercial product, mix a half-pound of complete fertilizer in four gallons of water. *Don't neglect to water transplants at least every other day for a week unless it rains.*

Heat and cold are the greatest dangers to transplants. The hardiest plant shifted from a windowsill to the open will wilt from the heat and probably die if exposed to direct sunlight. Transplanting should be done either in the early evening or on a cloudy day. Moreover, newly set plants must be shaded for a few days.

Newspaper tents, orange crates, and bushel baskets make excellent coverings for transplants. The various "caps" sold in garden centers also shield transplants from the sun and wind. Made of clear plastic, these devices are apt to blow away if not securely anchored. Moreover, on sunny days the air inside them may become so hot that the transplants wither and die. Thus, if the weather turns unseasonably warm, it is necessary to lift the caps every morning and replace them at night until all danger of frost is past.

Heat build-up poses no problem when capless, bottomless plastic gallon jugs are used as covers. Nor will the jugs blow away if soil is heaped around them. However, most gallon jugs made of plastic are opaque and plants protected by them receive no sunlight. Thus, they cannot be used for more than a few days except to cover plants at night.

6

GROWING SPECIFIC VEGETABLES

"There is always a right way to do anything. . . ."

Have you ever counted all the different vegetables displayed in a large supermarket's produce department? If so, the total probably amazed you. However, it is safe to assume that the store did not offer every food plant that is classified as a vegetable.

Actually, there are so many different vegetables that no book the size of this one could give directions for raising all of them. There is room here only to discuss those commonly raised by amateur gardeners. Moreover, because of the lack of space, unless a vegetable requires special protection from diseases or insects, no mention is made of the use of insecticides or fungicides. Such information is given in the section dealing with chemical dusts and sprays in Chapter 7.

For convenience, crops are listed in alphabetical order. To aid in seed selection, every entry includes the names of certain of the varieties most frequently recommended by agricultural experts throughout the United States. No attempt has been made to give specific cultural directions for limited areas. All the vegetables mentioned can be raised in practically any region. However, because of the differences in growing seasons, mention is made of the times to sow certain seed in the North and in the South.

Finally, parenthesized figures indicate the average number of days from sowing to harvest, with the exception of vegetables started under cover. Figures after "transplants" represent the average number of days from the setting out of started plants to maturity.

Because the pods of freshly picked bush beans (left) make a noise when broken, they are called "snap beans." Commonly called "wax" beans (right) because of their color, yellow bush beans are easily grown in any well-drained soil.

Beans

There are several varieties of beans. Those that climb are called pole beans, low-growing strains are known as bush or snap beans. The latter name is derived from the noise made when the freshly picked pods are broken. Despite the fact that seedmen have developed beans with stringless pods, snap beans are commonly called "string beans."

Green or yellow (wax) snap beans are the most popular varieties with backyard gardeners. Both kinds are prolific and easy to grow. Contender (48), Harvester (60), Tendercrop (53), and Tendergreen (56) are among the best green snap beans. Pencil Pod Wax (54) has long been a favorite yellow bush bean, and Burpee's Brittle Wax (54), Resistant King-horn Wax (54), and Cherokee Wax (52) are also widely grown.

All beans are tender and cannot be planted in cool areas until the ground has warmed. On the other hand, snap beans do not thrive in the lower southern and southwestern states in midsummer. But they can be grown successfully in both regions during fall, winter, and spring.

Both pole and bush beans flourish in any well-drained soil. While pole beans benefit from side-dressing after they set blossoms, bush beans require no additional feeding if planted in a garden that has received an application of complete fertilizer. However, if a second planting of beans is made in the same row from which a crop has been harvested, fertilizer should be worked into the soil before sowing

Bush beans should be planted in furrows approximately three inches wide, four inches deep, and at least two feet from adjoining rows. Space seeds about three inches apart and cover with soil tamped down with the back of a hoe. Take pains not to plant the seeds too deep—they should not be covered with more than an inch of heavy soil or an inch-and-a-half of light, sandy soil. When the seedlings emerge, begin cultivating and gradually fill in the furrow so that it is level with the rest of the garden.

Bean seedlings have difficulty pulling their folded leaves through soil that crusts when it dries out after a rain. As noted, you can help the young plants break through the ground by covering seeds with a mixture composed of equal parts of peat moss and sand instead of soil.

Because pole beans grow vertically they are an ideal crop for small vegetable gardens. Pole beans will climb fences, trellises, or the side of a porch. In gardens, pole beans are planted in hills spaced three feet apart

Although lima beans require a longer and warmer growing season than bush beans, they will not set pods in extremely hot weather.

and grown on supports. The best supports are trimmed saplings. Not only are they sturdy but also the vines cling to the bark, anchored by their spirally coiling tendrils. Light, narrow pieces of wood can be used as poles, but it is best to tie three or four of these together at the top with wire and to extend their lower ends so that a "wigwam" is formed. This arrangement makes the supports more substantial.

If poles are used they must be set deep enough to prevent their blowing over and should measure seven feet from the ground to their tops. Place poles in the middles of the hills *before* sowing seed.

The brown-seeded and white-seeded Kentucky Wonder (60) are the best varieties of pole snap beans. Drop six to eight seeds in a circle around each pole. When the seedlings are three inches tall, thin them, leaving only four plants to mature. Throw the thinnings on the compost pile.

Cultivate beans frequently to keep weeds down and to break up surface crust. Because all the seeds in the pods will not develop if the soil dries out, beans must be watered during dry spells.

Old-time gardeners avoid touching moist bean plants. This is because standard varieties have a tendency to rust if anything touches them when their leaves are wet. However, rust is rarely a problem if rust-resistant strains are planted. Similarly, growing varieties resistant to mildew and mosaic will reduce the chances of infection by these diseases. But no bean plant can withstand the depredation of bean leaf beetles or Mexican bean beetles.

Pick pole or bush snap beans as soon as they are big enough to eat. Young, tender pods have a better flavor and texture than old, large ones, and very young pods are delicious eaten raw right off the vine. Wax beans are at their peak when they turn a buttery yellow. Pole beans should be harvested before the seeds develop fully and round out the pods.

Daily pickings will prolong the life and productivity of bean plants. But the best way to insure a summer-long supply of tender bush beans (oversized pods can be dried and their seeds used for baked beans) is to make succession plantings. These should be sown every two weeks from the time the soil warms until seven weeks before the average first frost date in your area.

Beets

No vegetable is more widely grown in home gardens than beets. There is good reason. Beets are easily raised, resistant to cold, practically disease free, rarely pestered by insects, and mature quickly if their simple needs are met. Moreover, a row of beets produces two crops—"greens" and edible roots.

Although beets are fairly tolerant of heat, they prefer cool weather. As a result, they are best grown in warmer regions during the fall, winter, and spring. In northern regions beets can be sown as soon as the ground can be worked and successive plantings made every two weeks until mid-August.

The faster beets grow, the better their quality. To mature quickly they require ample water and fertile soil. But even if a garden is watered frequently and enriched with fertilizer, beets will not thrive unless the soil has a high content of organic material. Nor will beets do well in acid soil. In fact, beets reveal the need to lime a garden. If beets are stocky and have dark, green leaves, there is no excess acidity in the soil. Spindly beets with mottled foliage indicate that the soil is acid.

There is little difference in the numerous varieties of beets except for the

Rarely preyed upon by pests or infected by disease, beets are widely grown by backyard gardeners. But they do not thrive in acid soil.

The old saying "red as a beet" is not always true. These are Burpee's Golden, a variety with yellow roots.

shape and color of the edible roots. However, in areas where downy mildew is prevalent—check with the Extension Service to see if this is true of your region—a strain of a standard variety resistant to this disease, which causes the leaves to curl up and die, should be planted. Elsewhere, Early Wonder (53) and Detroit Dark Red (60) will prove satisfactory. If you want to try "something different," plant Burpee's Golden (55)—its roots are yellow. However, they taste no different than those of other beets.

Because beet seeds are actually balls composed of several individual seeds, they should not be sown thickly, despite the fact that beet seeds germinate poorly. Sow eight seeds to a foot in a shallow furrow made with a hoe handle. Cover the seed with compost or humus-rich soil and tamp it down firmly. A gentle sprinkling will stimulate germination. To retain moisture and to prevent the soil from drying out and caking, cover the row with lawn clippings or other material that will not bake. After the seeds sprout this mulch can be removed.

As soon as the young plants are established they must be thinned or they will not make proper growth. Thin seedlings to stand four inches apart unless you intend to harvest beet greens. If you do, thin to two inches. Then, when the plants are six to eight inches tall, thin again and use the pulled plants for greens.

When beets mature, the tops of the roots break through the soil. But many gardeners do not wait until beets are about two inches in diameter to harvest them, preferring "baby beets" to fully grown ones. Not only are baby beets delicious but pulling them gives the plants left in the row more room to develop. But when beets get too large they are fibrous and tough. The best thing to do with them is to throw them on the compost pile.

Cabbage

Cabbage can be grown practically anywhere in the United States. It is adapted to a wide variety of soils, providing they are fertile and moist. Although cabbage does best in cool weather, it can be grown in all seasons in the lower South except summer. Because cabbage is hardy, it can be set

Adaptable to a wide variety of soils, cabbage can be grown practically everywhere in the United States.

Broccoli, like all members of the cabbage family, must be planted in a different part of a garden every year to prevent infection from soil-borne diseases.

out in the fall as far north as Washington, D.C., overwintered without protection, and harvested the following spring.

In northern states an early cabbage is planted in the spring and a late variety set out in midsummer. Earliana (60), Early Jersey Wakefield (63), and Golden Acre (64) are best for spring planting. Copenhagen Market (72) and Danish Ballhead (105) are outstanding late strains. Red Acre (75) is an excellent red cabbage.

Early cabbage plants can be purchased or raised indoors. In either case choose a variety resistant to yellow blight. This disease, commonly called "yellows," is transmitted by bacteria that enter the roots near the stem. While aphids, cabbage loopers, cutworms, and other insects that feed on cabbage can be controlled by dusts and sprays, there is no cure for yellow blight.

After hardening off, early cabbage can be transplanted outdoors as soon as the ground can be worked. Space plants eighteen inches apart in rows two feet apart. When the transplants are established, give them a side-dressing of fertilizer with a high nitrogen content. Cabbage is a heavy feeder and each plant should receive an application of one-third of an ounce of fertilizer every three weeks. When well-fertilized, cabbage not only matures quickly but also has a better flavor, providing it never suffers from a lack of water.

Sow late cabbage seed outdoors in one-half-inch deep furrows. As soon

74

as the young plants develop their second set of leaves, thin the row and transplant the excess seedlings. Because late cabbage has larger heads than early varieties it must be spaced two feet apart and be three feet from the nearest row. It is not necessary to give late cabbage supplementary feeding.

Both early and late cabbages are ready to harvest when the heads are solid. The heads of mature early strains are apt to split in warm weather. Wetting the soil around the plants and twisting their stems so that some of the roots are broken will retard splitting.

Cabbage and its relatives—broccoli, brussels sprouts, and cauliflower—are susceptible to several soil-borne diseases. Their symptoms are easily identified: stunted growth, discolored foliage, and root swellings. Avoid soil-borne diseases by planting members of the cabbage family in a different part of a garden every year. If, despite this precaution, the soil becomes infected, do not raise cabbage or any of its kin for at least three years.

Carrots

Southern gardeners grow carrots throughout the fall, winter, and spring. In northern areas they are sown as soon as the soil has been prepared and succession plantings are made at three-week intervals until the latter part of July.

Carrots vary in shape and size. Short to medium-sized varieties are best for heavy soils. The long, slender strains thrive in light, loose, sandy soil. Short 'n Sweet (68) and Oxheart (75) are excellent stubby carrots. Red Cored Chantenay (70) and Spartan Bonus (75) are popular medium-length varieties. For long roots, plant Imperator (75), Gold Pak (76), or Nantes (70).

Sow carrots in a shallow furrow made in well-drained soil at a depth of not more than half an inch. Space plantings eighteen inches from other rows. After covering the seed, tamp the soil lightly, and water to stimulate germination. It may take nearly three weeks for seedlings to emerge. By the time they appear the row will probably be a carpet of weeds, making it impossible to locate the furrow planted to carrots. Mixing quickly germinating radish seed will mark the furrow and enable you to weed the row. Moreover, the radishes can be eaten when they are big enough. But before

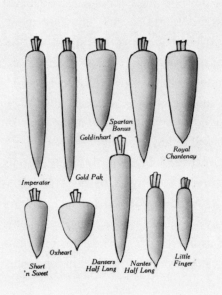

Labels on the illustration:
Spartan
Bonus

Goldinhart

Royal
Chantenay

Imperator

Gold Pak

Oxheart

Little
Finger

Short
'n Sweet

Danvers
Half Long

Nantes
Half Long

Long-rooted carrots should be planted in light, sandy soils. Short and stubby rooted varieties are the best carrots to raise in heavy soils.

mixing radish and carrot seed to combat weeds you must be able to distinguish their foliage. The easiest way to learn what their leaves look like is to visit a market.

As soon as carrots are an inch tall they must be thinned. Later thinnings are made when the tops of the greenish-yellow roots can be seen breaking through the soil. Harvesting the larger roots will thin the remaining plants and give them more room. When pulling carrots grasp the foliage close to the soil so that they will not break.

Carrots require no special care. Nor are they subject to insect attack. If an occasional carrot caterpillar (identified by black and yellow markings on its two-inch-long body) is seen chewing on the feathery leaves, pick it off by hand.

Cauliflower

Cauliflower is far more difficult to raise than cabbage. It will not head in warm weather. Thus it cannot be grown as a summer crop in the South. In northern regions, started plants must be kept under cover until all danger of frost is past.

With the exception of Purple-Head (85) which turns green when cooked, most varieties of cauliflower are improved strains of the standard Snowball which was developed years ago. Most experts recommend the planting of either Early Snowball (60) or Snow King Hybrid (50) in backyard gardens.

Except in the South, cauliflower should be started indoors about six weeks before outdoor planting time. After hardening transplants, set them two feet apart and two feet from the nearest row. Sprinkle a heaping teaspoonful of high-nitrogen fertilizer around each plant from time to time to aid vigorous growth. Give cauliflower a thorough soaking every week— it demands a great deal of water.

When the white buds are about the size of a half-dollar, lift the lower leaves and tie them together over the buds with soft twine or a rubber band. This will keep out the light and blanch the head. Examine cauliflower every three or four days. When the buds are firm, bone white, and approximately six inches in diameter, the heads are ready to harvest.

Chard

This easily raised vegetable's true name is Swiss chard. Actually a beet developed for its tops rather than for its roots, chard thrives in hot weather. As a result, it is widely planted for greens. The leaves may be prepared like spinach, the heavy midribs of the leaves like asparagus, or both cooked together.

The thick, dark green leaves and broad white stalks of Fordhook Giant (60) make it the most popular variety of chard. If the outer leaves are picked off a couple of inches above the crown when the plants are eight or ten inches high, new foliage replaces them. As a result, chard can be harvested all summer.

Chard resents acid soil. It also demands a constant supply of nutrients which are furnished by supplementary applications of nitrogenous fertilizer. The culture of chard is similar to beets but it must be thinned more. Pull plants for greens until those that remain stand a foot apart. Thinning

Fordhook Giant (left) is a "cut and come again" variety of Swiss chard. When the outer leaves are picked, new foliage replaces them. To really appreciate the taste of sweet corn (right), it should be eaten within minutes of being picked. The ears pictured here have yellow kernels— the variety favored by most backyard gardeners.

should begin when chard is four inches tall.

Leaf-sucking and chewing insects that prey on the cabbage family also attack chard. Toxic sprays used to control them should not be used within three days of picking "a mess of greens."

Corn

As indicated, corn produces a very small harvest for the amount of space it requires. But no vegetable is as tasty as sweet corn picked and eaten within a span of twenty minutes. Therefore, try to find room for at least a small planting of corn.

It would take several bushel baskets to hold all the varieties of corn. Some strains bear yellow kernels, others white. Still others have white and yellow kernels on the same ear. There are also varieties with kernels colored red, yellow, orange, and blue.

Moreover, the ears differ in size. Some ears are only four or five inches in length. These midgets are dwarfed by the eight-to-nine-inch ears of standard varieties.

Most gardeners consider Golden Cross Bantam (85) the finest of yellow sweet corn and Silver Queen (92) the best of white sweet corn. Honey and Cream (76), with its combination of white and gold kernels, is also very popular. Actually, any variety of freshly picked corn is delicious and you won't make a mistake by selecting any strain suitable for planting in your area.

Corn is difficult to raise in the South during the summer. But it thrives in the North when days are sunny and nights are warm, providing it gets plenty of moisture. In large gardens both an early and a late crop should be planted to insure a constant supply of ears.

Sow corn in hills or short rows three feet apart. Plant the seed thickly about one inch deep in rich soil. When the sprouts appear, thin out the weaker ones. Leave only three seedlings in hills and space them approximately ten inches apart in rows.

Corn requires a great deal of nourishment. When the stalks are a foot high scatter a complete fertilizer around them and rake it into the soil. To preserve moisture and to keep down weeds, cultivate frequently. While cultivating, hill soil around the stalks. This will support them and prevent their being blown over in high winds. Avoiding cultivating close to the stalks—corn roots lie close to the surface and are easily injured.

Sweet corn is ripe when the ears become plump and firm and the "silk" at their ends dries and turns black or a rusty brown. Ripe ears allowed to remain on the stalk become tough. Because corn loses some of its sugar content within seconds of being harvested, start heating water to cook corn before gathering it. To detach ears from stalks, hold them by the base and break them off with a quick downward twist.

Stripped stalks should be pulled. Otherwise, they will continue to draw nutrients from the soil. Corn stalks make excellent compost but take a very long time to decompose unless they are shredded.

Watch for the European corn borer and the earworm. The latter chews through the silk and damages kernels near the ear's tip. Earworms can be thwarted by squirting two or three drops of mineral oil into the ears with an eyedropper. Make the first application after the silk appears and repeat at least four times at two-day intervals.

Tiny holes in the sides or the base of ears indicate that corn borers have invaded your corn patch. They can either be picked off by hand or dusted with Sevin. This dust contains carbaryl, an insecticide that has replaced DDT. To prevent infestation by borers, start applying Sevin to the foliage when the stalks are eighteen inches high. Dust two or three times at five-day intervals. Because borers—the larvae of a night-flying moth—hibernate in dry stalks, destroy all stalks pierced by them. If this is not done you may find borers in your garden the following year not only feeding on the corn but also on other vegetables.

Cucumbers

Although a warm weather crop, cucumbers cannot tolerate heat. Wherever summer temperatures are high they must be planted only in the spring and fall. Cucumbers are also sensitive to cold. As a result, they are raised in the Deep South during the winter months and shipped to markets in the North.

Cucumbers vary greatly in size and shape. Some varieties have been developed for table use, others for pickling. Burpee Hybrid (60) can be employed for both purposes. Marketmore (67) is an excellent slicing cucumber, while Pioneer (51) is suitable for making all types of pickles.

Plant cucumbers either in hills or rows. Hills should be five to six feet apart and rows spaced the same distance. Because cucumbers require rich, mellow soil, well-rotted manure, organic matter, or commercial fertilizer must be placed at the bottom of the hills or furrows and covered with soil before seed is sown. Drop six to eight seeds in each hill and space seeds six inches apart in rows and cover to a depth of half an inch. When the plants are about six inches high, thin, leaving three or four in a hill and at least a foot between plants in rows.

While picking cucumbers look for fruit hidden by the leaves. If they are not harvested, the plants may stop producing. Large, yellow-green cucumbers indicate that they are overripe. To keep the vines bearing, pick mature fruit every two or three days.

Cucumbers vary greatly in size and shape. Long cylindrical varieties like the one pictured at right are best for slicing. Not only are hybrid varieties of cucumbers (below left) more prolific than standard strains, but also they are disease resistant.

Cucumbers developed for pickling (above right) can be harvested at any stage of growth. They are picked when the right size to make a particular kind of pickle. Gardening is more fun if part of a plot is used to raise unusual vegetables. Why not plant a few hills of lemon cucumbers (right)?

Cucumber foliage temporarily wilts on hot days. But the vines stop growing during dry spells. Merely sprinkling cucumbers will not supply the moisture they need. Because their roots may extend downward as much as three feet, the soil must be soaked. When watering, avoid wetting the leaves. The vines are more susceptible to disease when moist. Planting varieties resistant to scab, mosaic, leaf spot, and mildew lessens the possibility of infection. Spraying with Malathion or dusting with Sevin will control the beetles that feed on cucumber leaves and spread disease. If you don't want to use a chemical pesticide, covering cucumbers with a cheesecloth netting held down with rocks or soil is a good defense against attacks by beetles. However, the netting must be lifted when cultivating or weeding. Avoid stepping on the trailing ends of the vines. If you do, the plants may die.

Eggplant

It takes between 100 and 140 days for eggplant seed to develop into fruit-bearing plants. While eggplant can be sown directly during the spring

Because Black Beauty (left) bears a large crop of plump purple fruit, it is the favorite eggplant of most gardeners. Eggplants have woody stems. The best way to pick them (right) is to cut them off the plants with pruning shears.

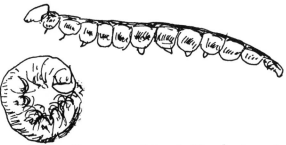

Cutworms shear plants off at ground level. The best protection against their ravages is to either wrap tinfoil around the stems of plants or to enclose the stems with a "collar" made of cardboard.

and fall in the South, started plants must be set out in northern gardens. Transplants can be either raised or purchased. When buying plants, check their stems. If they are "woody" (hard), the plants are not likely to produce well.

Selecting eggplant seed can be confusing. Some catalogs list over two dozen varieties. Most are standard, disease-resistant strains, but there are also those that bear green, yellow, or white fruit. Perhaps the best variety to grow in short-season areas is Early Beauty Hybrid transplants. They will yield an abundance of short, oval, dark purple fruit sixty-two days after being set in the garden. The most frequently recommended large-fruited eggplant is Black Beauty. Transplants will produce in seventy-five days.

Eggplant seed sown indoors should be planted about eight weeks before transplanting time. Set transplants eighteen inches apart in rows three feet apart. Cover them on cold nights. Eggplant cannot tolerate low temperatures. It becomes stunted in cool weather and does not make the quick growth necessary to produce quality fruit.

In well-fertilized gardens eggplant requires no supplementary feeding. However, it must be kept free of weeds and watered frequently. The plants will bear fewer but bigger fruit if late-appearing blossoms are pinched off immediately. Don't wait for the fruit to become overly large. Eggplant tastes best when not fully developed. You can tell when the fruit is at its peak by pressing it on the side with the ball of the thumb. If the skin does not spring back, pick the fruit.

A swarm of insects dine on eggplant. The most pesty is the eggplant lace

Containers in which individual transplants are growing can be easily transformed into "collars" to prevent damage by cutworms.

bug. Its presence is indicated by the browning and yellowing of the foliage. A Malathion spray will destroy lace bugs, providing it hits the undersides of the leaves. To prevent cutworms from shearing off eggplants—or any other vegetable—either wrap tinfoil around the stems or circle them with a collar two or three inches high made from a milk carton.

Lettuce

Lettuce is a cool-weather crop. It has a tendency to bolt (set seed) in the heat of summer, although certain varieties are more or less heat resistant. Nevertheless, it is difficult to raise lettuce during the summer except in far-northern areas.

There are four kinds of lettuce. Beginning gardeners should consider planting only the loose-leaf type. It does well in any nonacid soil enriched by a commercial fertilizer containing a large percentage of phosphorus. The chief merit of leaf lettuce is that it can be harvested over a long period. If the tender outer leaves are picked, they are soon replaced by new ones that sprout from the plants' centers.

Slobolt (45), Salad Bowl (40), and Black Seeded Simpson (44) are the most popular varieties of loose-head lettuce. You can get an extra early crop of any of these strains by starting seeds indoors and setting out plants when they have four or five leaves. Hardened lettuce can withstand tem-

Butterhead lettuce is two-toned. Its loosely folded outer leaves may be green or brownish, the inner leaves cream or the color of butter.

A novice gardener who successfully raises head lettuce has a right to boast. The variety pictured is Iceberg, which is the lettuce of commerce.

Green Ice is a most appropriate name for this strain of loose head lettuce. Its attractively crinkled leaves are a cool green.

peratures as low as 28° F. Outdoors, seed can be sown as soon as the soil has been tilled. Scatter a dozen seeds to the foot in shallow furrows eighteen inches apart and cover with one-half inch of soil. Rows should be short and successive plantings made every ten days except in midsummer. Resume sowing seed after days and nights become cooler.

Thin lettuce to four inches between plants when it is two inches tall. Be careful not to injure the roots of neighboring plants and don't throw away the "thinnings"—use them for salads. After thinning, scratch a small amount of nitrogenous fertilizer along the row. If weather conditions are favorable and the plants get sufficient moisture, this feeding will encourage growth and make another thinning necessary. Now the plants should stand ten inches apart. They'll grow faster if given a boost with an application of fertilizer from time to time.

Cabbage loopers and aphids attack lettuce. Because chemical residues are difficult to wash off lettuce leaves, pick the loopers off by hand. A stream of water from a garden hose will evict aphids.

Melons

Classified as a vegetable and eaten as a fruit, muskmelons (cantaloupes) have the same cultural requirements as cucumbers. However, melons are not as hardy as cucumbers and also demand more room.

Cantaloupe needs a long growing season. In cold regions seed must be started indoors three or four weeks before outdoor planting time. Pride of Wisconsin (92) is an excellent home variety, but in some areas either Saticoy Hybrid (90) or Samson Hybrid (90) may be a better choice. Both are resistant to powdery mildew and fusarium wilt. These diseases—which are widespread in certain areas—along with aphids and cucumber beetles often cause crop failure.

In long-season regions, melons can be sown outdoors either in hills or rows six feet apart. Drop six to eight seeds in each hill or scatter seed thinly in rows. After the plants are established, thin to three plants in a hill and space them twelve inches apart in rows. When the vines have "run" a foot, apply fertilizer around them. Give another feeding when the first melons are set. Water heavily until the fruit starts to ripen.

Because of its delightful aroma and flavor, the breeder of this hybrid cantaloupe aptly named it Ambrosia.

Some individuals claim they can tell when a muskmelon is ready to pick by its odor. Actually, the best way to determine if muskmelons are ripe is to lift them gently. If their stems break, they are ripe.

Watermelons not only demand more room than muskmelons but also they require warmer temperatures and far more fertilizer. But they are fun to grow.

Charlestown Gray (85) is a good variety for southern gardens. Resistant to wilt, fungus, and sunburn, its fruit weighs approximately thirty pounds. Northern gardeners should plant New Hampshire Midget (70) or another "icebox" type.

With the exception of allowing more room for vines to spread, the culture of watermelons is the same as that of muskmelons. Both are preyed upon by the same insects and are susceptible to the same diseases.

Onions

Although onions resent extremes of heat and cold, they are adaptable to a wide range of climatic conditions. But onions will not do well unless they are planted in nonacid, well-prepared, moist, friable, fertile soil that is free of clods and stones.

Onions can be raised from seed, started plants, or sets. The latter are small dry onions grown the previous year. Sets produce mature roots sooner than started plants which, in turn, take less time to mature than seed-grown onions.

Purchasing sets or plants has one disadvantage—the variety you want may not be available. Most sets are either yellow or white globe-shaped onions, while the majority of started plants are strains of the larger, sweet Spanish type. By planting seed one can choose between round, flat, gobular, or spindlelike onions with flesh differing in color and pungency. Then, too, seeds are far less expensive than either plants or sets.

However, if you decide to raise onions from seed, bear in mind that it will take approximately one hundred days for sizable bulbs to form. Even then, you may get a poor crop. Seed-sown onions often develop seed-stalks instead of large roots.

Onion seed can be planted early in the spring. Scatter twelve to fifteen seeds to the foot in a shallow furrow two feet from the nearest row and cover them with half an inch of soil. Started plants (they can be raised in flats) can also be set out early. Plant them four inches apart and two inches deep.

Sets are sold by the pound. Because large sets may produce seeds rather than bulbs, only buy sets that range between one-half and three-quarters of an inch in diameter. Sets are easy to plant. First, make a furrow two or three inches deep and refill it with soil. Then firmly press the sets into the soil two inches apart.

Cultivate onions frequently and keep them free of weeds. When plants are six inches high, side-dress with 5-10-10 fertilizer. Thin by pulling immature bulbs throughout the growing season. This will not only give the remaining plants more room but also furnish a supply of "green onions." If flower stalks appear, pinch them off so that seeds will not develop. Onions

The roots and stems of bunching onions are blanched by heaping soil against the plants.

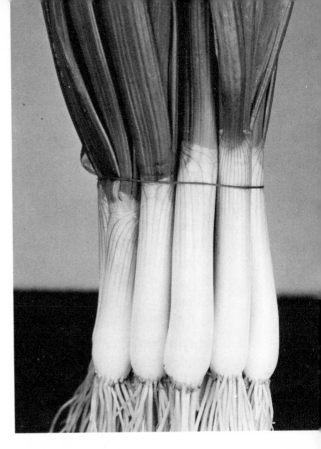

are ripe when their tops dry and flop. Ripening can be speeded up by bending down the tops of large bulbs. After harvesting onions, spread them out in the shade for a day or two to cure, then store in a dry, well-ventilated place.

Thrips and the onion maggot can be controlled by chemicals. Organic gardeners claim that the damage caused by the onion maggot can be eliminated by planting radishes along both sides of onion rows. Theoretically, instead of burrowing into the onions, the white, legless maggots will attack the radishes, which are pulled up and destroyed.

Peas

For decades similar objects have been described as being "alike as two peas in a pod." This statement is not true. When dried, some peas are smooth, others (these strains are the sweetest) are wrinkled.

These are three types of peas: green peas, edible-pod peas (sugar peas), and cowpeas. Green peas and edible-pod peas are cool weather crops and should be planted as soon as the ground can be worked. Cowpeas, brought to the New World from Africa by slave traders, require warm days and nights and cannot withstand the slightest frost. However, the culture of all three types of peas is the same.

The list of green peas in most seed catalogs is a long one. It includes bush dwarf varieties that can be raised without staking, and strains whose vines grow as much as six feet high. The latter varieties must be supported with chicken wire, brush stuck in the ground, or by a trellis.

Perhaps the best producers of fine quality peas on dwarf vines are Little Marvel (53) and Progress No. 9 (60). The latter is the earliest long-pod pea but some gardeners plant Alaska (55) because it matures so quickly, even though the small, round peas borne on its two-foot vines have little sugar content.

Among the best of the taller growers are Wando (68), which is not only resistant to cold but also tolerant of heat, and Freezonian (63). Thomas Laxton (65), a heavy cropper, has been a favorite for years because it does well under a wide variety of conditions.

Dwarf Gray Sugar (65) is the earliest and best of bush type edible-pod peas. Burpee's Sweetpod (68) is an outstanding tall growing strain producing prolifically on its four-foot vines.

All peas demand fertile soil. After digging a furrow six inches deep and four inches wide, scatter a low-nitrogen commercial fertilizer along the trench and cover it with four inches of soil or fill the furrow with four inches of compost.

Peas are usually planted in double rows—the supports for tall vines being placed between them. Drop the seed two inches apart and cover with two inches of soil. When the seedlings emerge, thin to stand three inches apart. Peas respond to frequent cultivation and also to a light side-dressing of complete fertilizer when they are about six inches high.

Green peas should be harvested when the pods are solid but the peas not full-sized. You can tell when peas are ready to pick by pressing pods between the fingers. If a pod feels firm, pick it.

Edible-pod peas should be picked as soon as the seeds begin to form, when the pods are still stringless. At this stage sugar peas can be cooked like snap beans. Mature edible-pod peas can be shelled—the large pods are too tough to eat. Cowpeas should also be harvested before the seeds get large and hard. Overripe pods should be shelled and the peas dried for future use.

Pea weevils and aphids prey on peas. As indicated, water will drive away aphids. While the tiny black, brown, or white weevils can be picked off by hand, spraying them with Malathion is easier. It also will get rid of the aphids.

Remember: Don't waste space! As soon as the last pea pod is harvested, pull the vines, prepare the soil, and sow a succession crop.

Peppers

There are two kinds of peppers: sweet and hot. Both are hot-weather plants. In cooler regions seed must be started eight to ten weeks before transplanting time. Gardeners in short-season areas should sow extra early strains of sweet peppers. These bear smaller fruit than the big bells borne by standard varieties but they mature much sooner. They are also more tolerant of high daytime temperatures and are not apt to drop their blossoms in excessively warm weather.

Vinette, Vinedale, and New Ace Hybrid are among the best extra early varieties of sweet peppers. Hungarian Wax is an excellent early hot pepper.

If left on the vines until they are fully matured, these "green peppers" will turn a brilliant red.

All these strains bear in approximately sixty-five days after being transplanted into a garden. Bell Boy Hybrid, Yolo Wonder, and Calwonder are popular standard varieties. They mature in about seventy days.

Set pepper plants in the least fertile section of a garden. Peppers develop more leaves than fruit when grown in rich soil. Place transplants two feet apart in rows spaced thirty inches. Once the plants set blossoms, they must receive a constant supply of moisture. If they do not, the blossoms will drop.

Never pull peppers off plants. Cut them with shears or a knife. While "green peppers" are delicious, the red, fully matured fruit is even more tasty.

Insects rarely bother peppers. However, plantings are sometimes invaded by leafhoppers and beetles. An application of an all-purpose spray will repel these pests.

Potato

For the amount of space it requires, the potato is one of the most productive of vegetables. A cool-weather crop (except for the dry fleshed "sweet" type), potatoes need a mellow, rich, well-drained soil. Heavy feeders, potatoes respond to liberal applications of either 5-10-10 or 5-8-7 commercial fertilizers but resent large amounts of lime.

Plant potatoes as soon as the ground can be worked. Some gardeners prefer to plant whole tubers. Others cut large sections containing at least two eyes from seed potatoes sold at garden supply stores or from old potatoes that have sprouted. While the latter practice saves money, purchasing seed potatoes insures that they are disease free.

Potatoes can be planted in hills or rows. Both hills and rows should be three feet apart and the whole potato or cut pieces sown in them spaced a foot apart. Spread fertilizer on the bottom of both hills and rows, cover it with three or four inches of soil, and plant both whole potatoes and sections at a depth of six inches. Heap a mound of soil over them.

When shoots appear in three or four weeks, cover them with soil. Repeat this chore until the plants are too big to bury. Meanwhile, cultivate between plants to eliminate weeds and to conserve moisture.

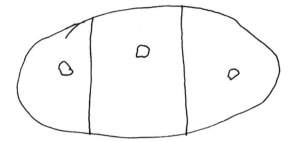

Old potatoes that have sprouted can be cut into sections and planted. Be sure each section has an "eye."

"Baby potatoes" may be dug as soon as they are big enough. But potatoes for storage should not be harvested until the tops of the vines die. Actually, the crop can be left in the ground for weeks unless the soil is saturated because of heavy rains. When digging potatoes, be careful not to jab them with the tines of a fork. Also avoid bruising potatoes intended for storage. Before storing, potatoes should be dried in the shade for a day or two.

Of all the pests that prey on potatoes, the worst is the Colorado potato beetle, commonly called the "potato bug." This avaricious insect devours the leaves, causing the plants to die. Either hand pick the adults, pink larvae, and egg-masses and drop them into a can containing kerosene or use a Malathion spray to get rid of all three.

Pumpkin

There is a special thrill eating a pie or making a Jack-o'-Lantern from a pumpkin one has raised. But unless trained to climb a fence, trellis, or wall, most varieties of pumpkins require far too much room to be grown in backyard gardens. This is because their vines run ten feet or more. However, seedmen have recently developed bush-type pumpkins that do not demand as much space as the standard varieties. Nevertheless, each plant needs approximately six square feet to develop properly.

The best of bush-type pumpkins are Cheyenne Bush (75) and Cinderella (95). Both bear fruit that is much smaller than those produced by vining types. Some of the latter produce pumpkins weighing more than one

The average backyard garden is not big enough to raise Big Max or other large pumpkins. However, there is usually room for a hill or two of the aptly named Jack-o'-Lantern variety.

hundred pounds! But the quality of these mammoths cannot compare to that of either Small Sugar (100) or Big Tom (120). Small Sugar is the best pumpkin for general use; Big Tom is best for canning and pies.

Affected by both heat and cold, pumpkins will not do well in northern regions when it is cool nor thrive in the midsummer heat of southern areas. Pumpkins cannot be planted until the soil has warmed. In short-season zones pumpkins can be started in pots and transplanted into the open when the weather has settled.

Sow six to eight seeds in hills from six to ten feet apart, depending on whether a bush or vining type is being planted. Cover seed with an inch of soil. When seedlings are established, thin the weaker ones, leaving two or three plants.

Because pumpkins sprawl in all directions—avoid stepping on plants and injuring them—weeding them is almost impossible. But mulching will keep down the weeds and, in addition, conserve moisture and keep the fruit clean.

Pumpkins have a better taste if they ripen on the vine. However, they should be harvested before a "hard" frost even if they have not matured, and left to ripen under shelter. When picking pumpkins leave part of the stem attached to the fruit. If weather permits, let pumpkins stay in the

deep. Thin seedlings when they emerge. Later thinnings will furnish tender greens for the table until the plants stand six inches apart. A side-dressing of nitrate of soda scratched in with a rake will spur growth.

Early in the season cut only the outside leaves. They will be replaced by new growth. When the weather becomes warm, pull entire plants. If left in the ground they will flower and set seed.

Actually, because of the difficulties in raising spinach, backyard gardeners who like "greens" will do better to grow either Swiss chard or a "summer spinach." These are tropical plants whose foliage is eaten as a vegetable. The best of these heat tolerant spinach substitutes are Tampala, New Zealand spinach, and Malabar spinach. A rapidly growing vine, Malabar spinach can be trained to climb.

Squash

Most seed catalogs list between twenty and thirty varieties of squash. But few backyard gardeners have enough room to raise winter squash—hard-shell squash that keep for months if stored in a cool, dry place—because winter squash grow on vines that send out runners eight to ten feet long. On the other hand, bush squash—commonly called summer squash—can be raised in hills spaced three or four feet apart.

Despite the fact that winter squash require a great deal of room, some gardeners with small plots raise Butternut (95), Hubbard (110), or Acorn (80). These individuals train the vines to climb fences, walls, or other sturdy supports. Winter squash can also be grown in a small garden if the runners are pruned after the vines have set fruit. However, this technique is risky—enough foliage must be left to feed the developing squash. Thus if you lack the means of growing winter squash vertically or are afraid of "scalping" vines, plant summer squash. The most popular variety is Early Pacific Straightneck (50) whose fruit can be harvested as soon as it is four inches long. Other popular summer squash are Early White Bush Scallop (60) and the various zucchini strains which bear long cylindrical yellow, green, gray, or black fruit in about sixty days.

Although slightly hardier than melons and cucumbers, squash are sensitive to frost. In short-season areas, winter squash can be started in peat

Zucchini blossoms (left), like those of all squash, can be eaten. Either fry them in a batter or stuff them with meat or cheese to make a most tasty dish. No squash pie tastes better than one made from a Blue Hubbard (right) raised in a backyard garden. But like all winter squash this long popular variety requires a great deal of room.

Butternut squash (left) can be grown in a small garden by either training the vines to climb a trellis or by pruning "runners" after fruit has set. Hubbard squash (right) is the finest of all winter varieties. Not only does its flesh have a delightful taste but also the hard shell makes it possible to store Hubbards for months.

Recipe for hungry gardeners: cut an acorn squash (below left) in half, remove seeds, pour maple sugar in the seed cavity, and bake until the squash is tender. Seed catalogs list this variety of summer squash (right) as Early White Bush, but gardeners refer to it as either Patty Pan or Scallop.

pots or berry boxes. After the last frost date, set three or four plants in well-fertilized hills spaced at least eight feet apart. When sowing seed of both vining and bush squash directly, plant six to eight seed in each hill about three inches apart. As soon as plants are established, thin winter squash to three to a hill and space summer squash at least a foot apart.

Bush varieties should be cultivated throughout the growing season. The hoeing of vining squash should stop when they send out runners. Actually, squash require no special care except for protection from the same pests that attack cucumbers and melons.

Summer squash should be picked when its skin can be punctured with the thumbnail. Winter squash must be left on the vine to mature, picked before the first "hard frost" with part of the stem attached, and stored in a cool place.

Tomatoes

Not all tomatoes are red. Some are orange, pink, or yellow. Tomatoes also vary in shape. Certain varieties resemble cherries, miniature plums, or pears. Others are globelike, round, or slightly flattened. There is also a difference in the size of the fruit. Tomatoes may be bite-sized or weigh over a pound. But no matter what their color, shape or size, tomatoes produce far more food in a small space than any other vegetable.

All tomatoes require warm weather, fertile soil, and ample moisture. However, some varieties take longer to mature than others. Buying started plants from a local source will insure getting a variety suitable to a specific area. Before raising tomatoes from seed, check with the nearest office of the Extension Service to learn which varieties do best in your region.

Originally a tropical plant, the tomato is very sensitive to frost. In most parts of the United States seed must be planted five to seven weeks before the time to set out transplants. Tomato seed germinates best at 70° F. As soon as seedlings are big enough to handle they should be shifted to flats or individual containers. Be sure to harden off plants before setting them in the garden.

Tomatoes "grown on the ground" produce more abundantly than supported plants. But they require more space, are difficult to cultivate, and

Yellow tomatoes (top left) contain almost the same amount of Vitamin C as red tomatoes, but some varieties are less acid than standard fruit. Whether eaten fresh or made into conserve, yellow plum tomatoes (top right) are delicious. Tomatoes (left) originated in the New World, but it wasn't until the mid-nineteenth century that Americans began to eat them. This hybrid strain of tomato (right) is resistant to verticillium and fusarium.

their fruit may rot because of contact with wet soil. As a result, most gardeners support tomatoes. The most common methods are tying the plants with strips of soft cloth to poles extending at least five feet above the ground or training the vines to climb a rope-and-wire trellis. The latter consists of two sturdy uprights connected at the top and base by strands of heavy wire to which vertical strands of twine are fastened. As the plants grow, their side shoots are pinched off and the main stalks twisted around the twine. If pruned to one stem—which reduces the quantity but increases the quality of the fruit—and supported, tomatoes may be set eighteen inches apart. Space unsupported vines four to five feet.

To transplant tomato plants:

1. Dig a two-foot hole.
2. Fill the hole with water and let it seep into the ground.
3. Scatter a scant handful of 5-10-10 fertilizer over the bottom of the hole and cover it with soil.
4. Set the transplant as deep as possible.
5. Tamp the soil around the transplant so that a water-holding depression is formed.

If tomatoes receive too much fertilizer they grow rank but bear little fruit. However, after the vines set fruit, a light application of high phosphorus content fertilizer should be worked into the ground around them with a rake. A second application ten days later will also prove beneficial.

Too much or too little water and insufficient sunlight will also keep tomato plants from fruiting. Moreover, the vines have a tendency to expend their energy growing instead of developing fruit. This can be overcome by removing the suckers—the tiny branches that appear between the stalk and side branches. If suckers are not removed, they sap the strength of the fruit-bearing main stem.

Nothing tastes better than a vine-ripened tomato. But green fruit remaining on plants when a heavy frost is threatened should not be discarded. Either pick and store the tomatoes in shallow boxes or hang the whole plants on a nail by their roots. Both boxes and vines should be kept in a cool, dark place. Eventually, most of the fruit will ripen.

Among the most common insects that attack tomatoes are white flies, various beetles, and the tomato hornworm. White flies can be checked with a Malathion spray, beetles and hornworms with either a Sevin spray or dust. To prevent infection by wilt or blight, apply a fungicide containing copper to tomato plantings.

7

GARDENING CHORES

"As you sow, so shall you reap"

According to the Bible there is ". . . a time to plant, and a time to pluck up that which is planted. . . ." However, because of climatic conditions, seeds are sown and crops are harvested at various times in different parts of the United States. When January's snows blanket the East and Midwest, gardening activity is limited to making plans and reading seed catalogs. Meanwhile, in the lower South, gardeners are setting out cabbage transplants and sowing the seeds of root crops and lettuce.

Planting and harvesting seasons may differ from one region to another but gardening chores are the same everywhere. Some are difficult. Others require very little effort. But all of them must be done. No garden will thrive without care, even if its soil is rich in nutrients and weather conditions are ideal.

Experienced gardeners work in their plots for a few hours each day. They not only find this less strenuous and tiresome than spending several hours once a week tending their plantings, but also a daily inspection enables them to check if watering is necessary and to control diseases, insects, and weeds before they get out of hand.

Weeding

Small weeds are easier to pull than large ones. Moreover, it is quite difficult to remove a large weed without uprooting nearby vegetable plants.

Therefore weeds should be pulled as soon as they emerge.

Hoeing between rows will eliminate many weeds. Those growing in rows or hills must be pulled by hand. The most comfortable way to do the job is to kneel or sit close to plantings. As you lift the weeds, toss them into a container so that you can dump them on the compost pile. Incidentally, if the tops of weeds break off while being pulled, it shows that the soil is dry and requires watering.

Cultivation

As indicated, hoeing between the rows will discourage weeds. Cultivation also prevents crusting, conserves moisture, gives plants support, and aids aeration by loosening soil. Plants will not develop roots unless air can move freely through the soil, carrying oxygen and removing carbon dioxide.

When cultivating do not dig too deeply—the roots of many vegetables lie close to the surface.

There is little danger of topsoils being washed away by heavy rains in a well-cultivated garden. Loose soil sops up water like a sponge. But keep cultivation shallow; hoe or rake with a sweeping motion when working near plantings.

Watering

Too much or too little water will kill vegetable plants. Ideally, the soil should be moist enough to dissolve nutrients so that the root hairs can absorb them in solution but should never be so wet that water fills the air spaces scattered through soil.

There is no definite rule for watering gardens. The frequency of waterings depends upon two factors: weather and the water-capacity of one's soil. Water drains slowly through soils with a high clay content but moves rapidly through light, loamy, or sandy soils. Therefore light soils have to be watered more often than heavy soils.

A garden can be watered in several ways. Individual plants can be given a "drink" with a watering can. Not only is this a time-consuming chore but also, unless a depression is made around the plants, the water will run off and little moisture will reach the roots. It is far less tiresome to water plantings with an automatic sprinkler or a hose. As indicated, a soaking hose is an excellent irrigation device. It also has the merit of not requiring attention. But it is not necessary to stand and hold an ordinary garden hose to water. Merely prop the hose's nozzle (adjusted to emit a fine spray) on a brick or rock, turn on the water, and leave. To prevent flooding, move the hose to a different location every twenty minutes. Although oscillating and rotating sprinklers also have to be moved from time to time, they provide the easiest method of watering a garden. In addition, mechanical sprinklers insure that the same amount of water falls on every section of a garden.

Irrespective of how a garden is watered, it should be soaked, not sprinkled. Deep watering stimulates roots to push downward where the soil is apt to be moist. Shallow watering encourages roots to remain close to the surface where they can be injured during cultivation or burned by the sun.

A sprinkler lightens the chore of watering a garden and also insures an even distribution of moisture. However, never sprinkle your plantings, soak them.

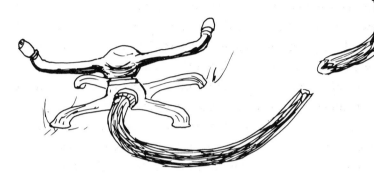

Generally speaking, a garden should be heavily watered once a week except during periods of heavy rains. Don't rush the job—in order for moisture to reach roots six to eight inches below the ground approximately one-and-a-half inches of water must fall on the soil.

The best time to water is early in the day. This allows plants time to dry completely before the sun sets. Dampness and darkness make vegetables more susceptible to disease.

Mulching

Dictionaries define a mulch as "any substance spread upon the ground to protect the roots of plants from heat, cold, or to keep fruits clean." Mulches also smother weeds, hold moisture, reduce the rotting of vine crops because of contact with damp soil, and prevent crusting.

There are two methods of mulching a garden. One is to spread hay, lawn clippings, peat moss, pine needles, sawdust, or other organic materials between the rows and around plants. Because organic mulches are decomposable and, when spaded under, enrich and improve the structure of soil, they are widely used.

The second method consists of mulching with clear or black polyethylene film. Sheets of both types are spread over the garden after the soil is prepared and anchored with stones along their edges. Cross-shaped slits allow seed to be sown or transplants set, while T-shaped openings permit water to reach the soil.

Both plastic and organic mulches have disadvantages as well as merits. Organic mulches applied early in the spring prevent the sun's rays from warming the soil. This increases the danger of transplants being nipped by a late frost. However, the seeds of hardy vegetables sown in beds covered with clear polyethylene germinate readily because the sun's rays penetrate the plastic and warm the soil under it. When the seedlings emerge, the film is removed. Then, after the young plants are thinned another sheet of plastic in which openings have been cut is placed around them.

While an organic mulch will stifle the growth of annual weeds, clear plastic stimulates their growth. Because black polyethylene blocks light, neither annual or perennial weeds sprout under it. Strangely enough, although black plastic does not warm soil as quickly as clear film, it not only hastens the maturing of warm weather crops in cool regions but also increases their yield.

Neither plastic nor organic mulches should be applied unless the soil is damp. Organic mulches can be spread between rows at any time. But they should not be placed around individual plants until the plants are approximately four inches tall.

When purchasing polyethylene for mulching buy the thickest film available. The depth of an organic mulch depends upon its composition. Mulches composed of coarse materials should be four inches thick; those consisting of fine materials only two inches deep.

If you plan to mulch with sawdust be sure to work one-fourth more fertilizer into your garden than its area demands. This will compensate for the loss of nitrogen in the soil as bacteria decompose the sawdust. Similarly, when pine needles are employed as a mulch, additional lime must be spread to compensate for the needles' acidity.

Dusting and Spraying

Insecticides and fungicides used to control insects and plant diseases are poisonous. In recent years environment-conscious gardeners have become greatly concerned about the effect chemical dusts and sprays have on wild-

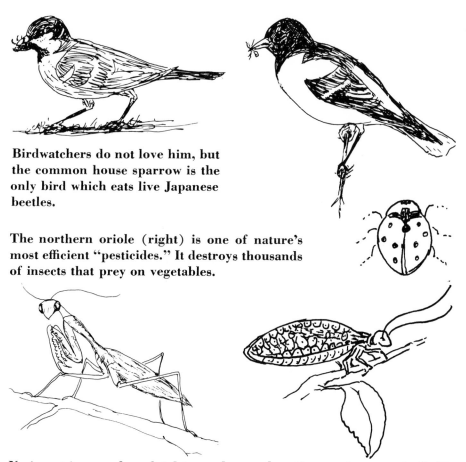

Birdwatchers do not love him, but the common house sparrow is the only bird which eats live Japanese beetles.

The northern oriole (right) is one of nature's most efficient "pesticides." It destroys thousands of insects that prey on vegetables.

No insect is more beneficial to gardeners than the praying mantis (left). Both the ladybug (right middle) and the lacewing (above right) destroy thousands of plant pests. A ladybug may eat as many as fifty insects a day. Lacewing larvae consume so many aphids that they are called the aphid lion.

life and man. Thus, instead of dusting and spraying with chemicals, some individuals hang praying mantis egg cases (available from seedmen) in sheltered parts of their gardens. When the young mantids hatch, they feed on aphids, flies, and other small insects. As adults, mantids dine on beetles, caterpillars, and similar large pests.

Organic gardeners also plant beans and potatoes close together. They claim that the beans repel the potato beetle and that the potatoes drive away the Mexican bean beetle. To thwart aphids, organic gardeners sow

**Organic gardeners claim that planting marigolds
in a vegetable garden drives away harmful insects.**

lettuce beside chives, repulse cucumber beetles by planting radishes in cucumber hills, and scatter stands of marigolds throughout their gardens. While the most unpleasant scent of marigold blossoms may not keep all destructive insects away from vegetable plants, their gay colors do make any garden more attractive.

Both organic gardeners and chemical users follow many of the same

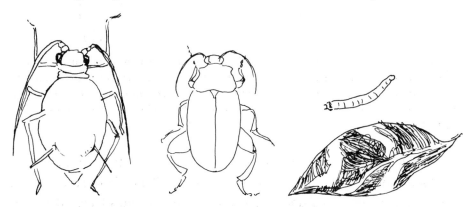

Aphids (left) prey on many different vegetables. Dousing them with a powerful stream of water usually will drive them out of a garden. "Buck-shot" holes in vegetable foliage are a sign flea beetles (middle) have invaded a garden. The holes not only weaken plants but also make them susceptible to disease. The narrow tunnels (right) that pierce the leaves of many vegetables are bored by the yellow larvae of the leaf miner.

gardening techniques. They immediately destroy diseased vegetation, remove plants from which a crop has been harvested so that they will not attract and shelter pests, and avoid water-borne diseases by staying out of their gardens in wet weather. All good gardeners also keep the grass near their plots closely trimmed. Long grass not only provides insects with cover but also it encourages the outbreak of certain diseases.

However, despite preventive measures, sooner or later most gardens are plagued by insects or disease. This means that every gardener must decide whether to use chemical or organic controls. Some individuals combine both methods.

Organic gardeners combat insects by hand-picking them off plants, dousing them with water, or by applying organic pesticides. They treat infected plants with organic fungicides. The sprays and dusts they employ are compounded from rotenone or from pyrethrum. Rotenone is derived from derris, a relation of the pea, while pyrethrum is extracted from certain chrysanthemums. Both rotenone and pyrethrum are relatively harmless to animals and man.

If you decide to fight insects and diseases with chemicals, use them with caution. Read labels carefully and follow directions. Wash your hands and face thoroughly when you finish spraying or dusting with any chemical pesticide or fungicide. Also avoid inhaling chemical dusts and sprays or getting them in your eyes, nose, or throat while mixing or applying them to plants. The accidental swallowing or breathing in of toxic chemicals is

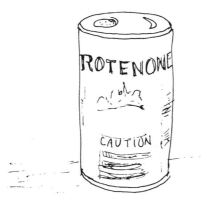

Nontoxic to man and animals (except fish), rotenone, an organic pesticide, controls most chewing and sucking insects.

greatly reduced if you do not spray or dust on windy days.

Sprays are best for disease prevention, dusts preferable for insect control. Dust requires no preparation. In addition to containing one or more pesticides (which makes them lethal to a variety of pests), many dusts also include a fungicide. Usually, sprays require mixing just before being applied. They are made by adding differing amounts of water to wettable powders or emulsified concentrates. Formulas for making chemical sprays of various strengths are given on the containers in which the powders or concentrates are sold. The insects each solution will kill are also identified.

It is impossible to spray or dust effectively without proper equipment. When buying a sprayer, choose one fashioned from noncorrosive metal and so constructed that it can be easily cleaned after each use. Also make sure that the nozzle can be turned in all directions—only those parts of a plant that are covered with chemicals are protected from infection or infestation.

The most durable and servicable dusters are the fan- or crank-type which hold up to fifteen pounds of dust. However, plunger-type dusters with capacities of one to three pounds are more practical for small gardens. Be sure the one you buy has a tube and nozzle attachment that allows dusting the underside of foliage.

8

CONTAINER GARDENING

"Good things come in small packages."

Many city dwellers are frustrated gardeners. One of their favorite sections of the Sunday newspapers is the Garden Section. Some of these individuals even subscribe to gardening magazines. As they read them, they envy those who have yards where they can raise vegetables.

However, one does not have to live in the suburbs or the country to have a vegetable garden. All vegetables can be grown in containers under artificial lights, or on balconies, terraces, windowsills, and the flat roofs of apartments and town houses. Of course, it is not practical to raise certain crops in an urban minigarden. A "hill" of corn planted in a container may delight visitors but a tomato plant will produce a more bountiful harvest.

Space may be more of a problem to container gardeners than to suburban "farmers," but urban gardening has its advantages. Transplants can be set out and seeds sown in containers long before outdoor plots can be turned over and soil is warm enough to encourage germination. This is because city temperatures average from five to ten degrees higher than suburban temperatures. Similarly, on cool nights while backyard gardeners rush to cover tender seedlings, container gardeners can bring their plantings indoors, close sliding glass doors, or place pots against a warm chimney. Then, too, during the growing season, containers can be moved from one part of a balcony, terrace, or rooftop to another so that they can receive more or less sunshine. It is also far less tedious to weed, cultivate, and water containers than long rows of vegetables. But the greatest merit of

111

**Seedsmen have developed miniature strains
of many vegetables for container gardening.**

container gardening is that it enables individuals who think they have no place to raise vegetables to experience the delights of "making things grow."

Obviously, available space determines the number of containers that can be planted. The size of the containers is regulated by the kinds of vegetables grown. For example, radishes, lettuce, and onions will thrive in ten-inch pots but tomatoes require containers with a capacity of one to three gallons of soil.

Containers

Most large department stores and all garden supply centers sell containers designed for holding plants. Varying in shape and size, these planters are fashioned from clay, metal, plastic, or wood. Many of them are extremely attractive and, as a result, add much to the appearance of a mini-garden. But commercial containers are usually quite expensive. You can save money and have fun by making your own containers. Any moisture-proof article can be transformed into a planter, providing it can be modified to drain and is large enough to hold a full-grown plant or plants.

Bushel and half-bushel baskets, wooden boxes, tubs, and galvanized pails are excellent "beds" for vegetables. If wooden containers are painted inside and out with a preservative, they will last for several years. Before buying any preservative, check to see if it is toxic to vegetation. This information will appear on the can's label.

Few factory-produced planters are as colorful as those made from plastic pails, trash cans, tubs, wastebaskets, or washbasins. Woven plastic laundry baskets can also be transformed into practical and charming containers by lining them with black polyethylene.

Whenever solid plastic articles are converted into planters, allowance must be made for drainage. At least four holes should be made in them. Space the holes evenly around the sides of the container just above the base. The best tool for this job is a red-hot spike held firmly in a pair of pliers. To heat the spike, lay it across a stove burner. To speed drainage through the holes put an inch or more of coarse gravel in all containers before filling them with loam or a soil substitute.

Holes drilled in the base of a wooden window box and gravel will pre-

Window box (left) with lettuce

Stair-step planter (below)

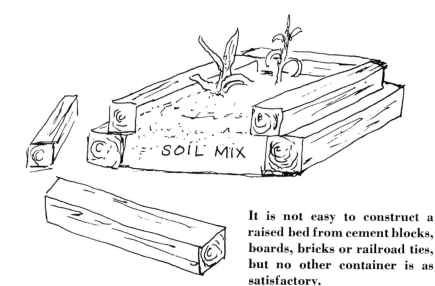

It is not easy to construct a raised bed from cement blocks, boards, bricks or railroad ties, but no other container is as satisfactory.

vent the soil in the box from becoming waterlogged. Stair-planters, which are merely stepped window boxes, require the same treatment. Gravel should also be placed in the bottom of hanging pots and plant baskets.

A soil enclosure constructed of boards, bricks, or concrete blocks is called a raised bed. These permanent structures are becoming increasingly popular with backyard gardeners whose plots contain more clay than humus. While a raised bed is an ideal "container," most minigardeners have good reason to think they are impractical on a terrace or roof. Not only are the materials needed to build raised beds expensive but also it is no easy task to carry them to the roof of an apartment house. Then, too, you'll have wasted time, effort, and money if you move!

Nevertheless, raised beds greatly increase the pleasures of gardening. They can transform a terrace or rooftop into a suburban backyard. Available space is the only limitation in their length, while location determines their width. If accessible from both sides, a raised bed can be six to eight feet wide. Beds situated so that they can only be tended to from one side should be about three feet wide. Training plants to grow vertically will compensate for the narrower area.

Irrespective of their length or width, all raised beds should contain at least a foot of soil. While this is enough soil to support any vegetable, constructing beds sixteen inches high turns them into a gardener's delight —they can be weeded while sitting in a chair. So can minigardens planted in deep wooden boxes set on sturdy tables.

Like all containers used for minigardening, raised beds, step-planters, and table-top planters do not place an undue strain on floors or rooftops. This is because they are not filled with ordinary soil but with a lightweight growing medium.

Synthetic Soil

Not only are soil substitutes extremely light in weight but also they contain no weed seeds or plant disease organisms. Moreover, they do not easily become waterlogged. Synthetic soils also maintain excellent aeration. Indeed, it is possible to use a package of synthetic soil as a waterproof planter. Merely cut slits in the plastic bag and either sow seed or set transplants through the openings.

Soil substitutes are sold under various trade names. Basically, all of them are the same. They are compounded from peat moss, fertilizers, agricultural lime, and either sand or vermiculite. If you are only going to plant a few containers it is best to buy one of the packaged mixes. However, if you need a large amount of synthetic soil it will be far cheaper to mix it yourself.

Synthetic Soil Formula

1 bushel of vermiculite

1 bushel of shredded damp peat moss

1 cup of 5-10-10 fertilizer

1¼ cups of agricultural lime

½ cup of superphosphate

(To make larger or smaller amounts of "soil" increase or decrease ingredients proportionally.)

Mix vermiculite and peat moss into a pile. Scatter fertilizers and lime over the pile and work them thoroughly into it. Make sure all ingredients are evenly distributed.

Radishes (left) can be grown in window boxes or in ten-inch pots. Be sure to water them frequently to insure rapid growth. Not only is rhubarb chard (right) delicious, but also its deep red stalks and crinkled lush green leaves make it a most attractive plant for a container garden.

Container Crops

Most seed catalogs list dwarf strains of vegetables. Generally speaking, these are more satisfactory for planting in containers than the standard varieties. Compact in growth, they take less room and also mature quickly. For example, Dwarf Morden, a midget cabbage whose flavor-filled heads are only four inches around, is ready to harvest in fifty-three days.

By looking for such descriptive names as Dwarf, Patio, Pixie, Small, or Tiny, you can spot seeds recommended for sowing in containers. But don't expect to find miniature strains of *all* vegetables listed in catalogs. Why would anyone wish to plant tiny radishes? Moreover, the standard varieties of radishes, beets, and lettuce are well adapted to growing in containers. So are carrots—particularly Little Finger and Short 'n Sweet, whose three-to-four-inch roots mature within sixty-five days.

Incidentally, planters containing carrots make an attractive border around a minigarden because of the plants' feathery foliage. Charming

116

effects can also be created by strategically placing plantings of Salad Bowl or Ruby Lettuce. Both these nonheading varieties are as handsome as they are tasty. Salad Bowl has bright-green curved wavy leaves while Ruby's frilled foliage is bright red. Rhubarb chard is another ornamental vegetable that does well in containers. Red veins run through its dark-green, heavily crumpled leaves, and the stalk resembles rhubarb.

The glossy leaves, bell-like blossoms, and the green, yellow, or red fruit of peppers also add color to a container garden. Both hot and the early varieties of sweet peppers should be planted in large tubs. Similarly, any of the nearly three dozen varieties of eggplant will produce an abundance of colorful fruit when grown in a good-sized container. However, the low-growing, large fruited strains are not as attractive in planters as strains bearing small to medium-sized fruit high on their stems. Among the best of the latter type are Morden Midget, Apple Green, Egg, and Golden Egg. Not only are the fruits of these varieties decorative but also they are delicious.

The contrast of deep red fruit against the lush green foliage of tomato

Cayenne peppers are not only a favorite seasoning of gourmet cooks, but also they make a decorative addition to the vegetable garden.

Full-grown tomato in pail or plastic wastebasket.

plants adds beauty to a container garden. Both standard varieties and miniature strains do well in planters. However, standard tomatoes must be raised in containers with a three-to-five gallon capacity. Strains developed for container gardening will thrive in smaller planters providing they receive frequent light applications of fertilizer.

Seedmen offer a number of "patio type" tomatoes whose vines and fruit vary in size. Among the most popular are Tiny Tim and Early Salad Hybrid. Tiny Tim rarely grows more than twelve inches tall and produces a rich harvest of cherrylike fruit. Early Salad Hybrid bears dozens of two-inch fruit on six- to eight-inch high vines that have a spread of approximately two feet.

Space Saving

When planting your minigarden don't forget that training vine crops to grow vertically against a trellis or other support saves space. So do hanging

118

containers. You can purchase complete units and hangers in garden supply shops or convert any plastic pot into a planter that can be hung with very little effort. Make three or four evenly spaced holes around the rim of a pot, fasten about two-and-a-half feet of picture wire to each hole, and twist the strands together at their ends. Equalize the lengths of all the wires and then bend them into a loop or a hook.

If you have room for only one hanging pot, raise Tiny Dill Cuke in it. Given ample sunshine and proper care, this dwarf will yield a tremendous crop of finger-length fruit on its two-foot vines.

Container Culture

With the exception of weeding, vegetables grown in containers filled with synthetic soil require the same care as those raised in the ground. They have to be watered, cultivated, fertilized, and protected from disease and insects.

Containers should be watered whenever the top one-eighth inch of soil is dry. In hot, dry weather it may be necessary to water planters three or more times weekly. But avoid overwatering. Use your sprinkling can as early in the day as possible—remember wet leaves and darkness encourage

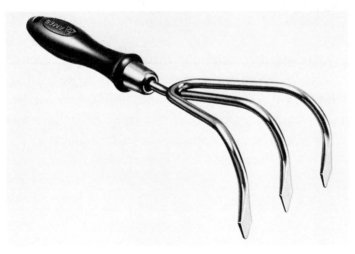

A trowel or hand cultivator will keep soil in containers from becoming compacted.

plant diseases. Of course, sowing resistant strains will lessen the chances of your plantings becoming infected.

At first thought it seems most unlikely that vegetables growing in a city container garden are subject to attack by the same insects that devastate backyard gardens. But high winds may bring a swarm of unwanted visitors to your minigarden. If this happens, use either chemical or organic controls.

The best way to cultivate plants in large containers is to use a trowel. Soil in small planters can be loosened with miniature garden tools. These gadgets—sold in department stores as well as garden shops—are most practical. But a large two-tined kitchen fork works just as well.

Because the vegetables growing in containers have restricted root space, they require more fertilizer than vegetables planted in the open. Give your containers frequent light applications of water soluble fertilizer rather than one or two heavy feedings. Don't fertilize when the containers are dry.

Take a Chance

Experts flatly state that a garden should produce the largest possible yield for the space it occupies. Technically, they are correct. But breaking the rules adds much to the joys of container gardening. Don't be afraid to raise "something different" even if it requires more space than you can spare.

Seed catalogs are crammed with challenges for container gardeners. Why not accept one? You might, for example, try to raise a crop of peanuts. Sow the shelled seeds—be careful not to injure the red "skin" that covers them—about two inches deep. When the seedlings emerge, water them regularly and give their containers as much sunlight as possible. In time, if all goes well, the plants will be covered with yellow flowers. As the blossoms wither, stalks extending from them will enter the soil and peanuts will form at their ends. The crop can be harvested after the plants turn yellow.

9

HARVEST TIME

"Whoso keepeth the fig tree shall eat the fruit thereof."

Legend holds that the gods of ancient Greece dined on ambrosia. If old tales are true, ambrosia not only was "exquisitely gratifying in taste and scent" but also it made those that partook of it immortal.

Any gardener who has raised cucumbers, lettuce, onions, green peppers, and tomatoes and made a salad from them has no need to envy the feasts of the gods on Mount Olympus. Of course, eating the crops one has grown does not guarantee eternal life, but freshly picked vegetables are delicious. Moreover, reaping a harvest from a backyard or container garden compensates for the disappointment if a garden did not reproduce the brilliant color pages in seed catalogs.

Similarly, a "mess of greens" or a liberally salted, heavily buttered, tender ear of sweet corn will completely erase all memories of cold, wet weather in spring, midsummer sweltering humidity, and rain-drenched weekends that not only dampened enthusiasm for gardening but also flooded plantings.

But freshly picked vegetables and crops canned, frozen, or stored in a cool, dark place for future use, are not the only rewards of gardening. It provides enjoyable exercise in the open air, furnishes an opportunity for one to forget the real and imagined situations that frustrate him, and, most importantly, allows a collaboration with Nature.

No one can deny that gardening involves an expenditure of time, money, and effort. But no leisure time activity is more rewarding. This is

A productive backyard garden

why, in late fall, many individuals recalling how much work their garden entailed and cost of seeds and fertilizer swear they will never sow another row as long as they live. However, when the mailman begins to deliver new seed catalogs in midwinter, most people who claim they are through with gardening, change their minds. Recalling only the joys of gardening they make out a seed order—and probably list twice as many varieties as they have room to grow!

STATE AGRICULTURAL EXPERIMENT STATIONS

ALABAMA
Auburn

ALASKA
College

ARIZONA
Tucson

ARKANSAS
Fayetteville

CALIFORNIA
Berkeley
Davis
Los Angeles
Parlier
Riverside

COLORADO
Fort Collins

CONNECTICUT
New Haven
Storrs

DELAWARE
Newark

FLORIDA
Gainesville

GEORGIA
Athens
Experiment
Tifton

HAWAII
Honolulu

IDAHO
Moscow

ILLINOIS
Urbana

INDIANA
Lafayette

IOWA
Ames

KANSAS
Manhattan

KENTUCKY
Lexington

LOUISIANA
Baton Rouge

MAINE
Orono

MARYLAND
College Park

MASSACHUSETTS
Amherst

MICHIGAN
East Lansing

MINNESOTA
St. Paul

MISSISSIPPI
State College

MISSOURI
Columbia

MONTANA
Bozeman

NEBRASKA
Lincoln

NEVADA
Reno

NEW HAMPSHIRE
Durham

NEW JERSEY
New
Brunswick

NEW MEXICO
Las Cruces

NEW YORK
Geneva
Ithaca

NORTH CAROLINA
Raleigh

NORTH DAKOTA
Fargo

OHIO
Columbus
Wooster

OKLAHOMA
Stillwater

OREGON
Corvallis

PENNSYLVANIA
University
Park

RHODE ISLAND	TENNESSEE	VERMONT	WEST VIRGINIA
Kingston	Knoxville	Burlington	Morgantown
SOUTH CAROLINA	TEXAS	VIRGINIA	WISCONSIN
Clemson	College Station	Blacksburg	Madison
SOUTH DAKOTA	UTAH	WASHINGTON	WYOMING
Brookings	Logan	Pullman	Laramie

INDEX